WHAT OTHERS ARE S
REFLECTIONS ON RISK II

"This second volume of Annie Searle's *Reflections on Risk* continues her tradition of bringing critical issues facing our society to the forefront through a careful combination of education, collaboration and inspiration. The essays in this book are a result of her mentorship and guidance of students in the University of Washington Master of Science in Information Management program at the University of Washington Information School, and provide a window into the varied and complex issues facing individuals and organizations as we move further into the Information Age. The background and insights provided in this work should be required reading for all; they illuminate the numerous and diverse challenges we face in managing and securing our information assets in the digital world, as well as providing a glimpse into the minds that will be shaping our future. "

- Michael Crandall, Senior Lecturer and Director, iAffiliates Program, *University of Washington Information School*

"Annie Searle's *Reflections on Risk, Volume II* shines a much-needed lens on a range of the most pressing issues facing all firms – both public and private – today from the phenomenon of big data, mobile payments and Bitcoin to the increasing

and ever-present threat of cybercrime in all industry sectors. The sheer range of current operational risk issues addressed in this book makes it required reading for all risk managers."
- Victoria Tozer-Pennington, Editor, *The Risk Universe.*

"A thought provoking collection of essays on risk management by Annie Searle and colleagues. *Reflections on Risks, Volume II* touches a range of contemporary topics from big data to mobile transactions and shines light on the risk management challenges facing organizations of all sizes and forms. The essays offer much to ponder and reflect for both novices and experienced risk managers."
- Kevin C. Desouza, Author, *Intrapreneurship: Managing Ideas within Your Organization*

REFLECTIONS ON RISK

VOLUME II

ASA INSTITUTE FOR RESEARCH AND INNOVATION

ANNIE SEARLE & ASSOCIATES LLC

EDITED BY EMILY OXENFORD

TAUTEGORY PRESS
SEATTLE, WASHINGTON

Printed in the United States of America

First edition: February 2014

Tautegory Press, Seattle, Washington USA

Printing History

All research notes here were previously published as "ASA Research Notes" in ASA Newsletters ©Annie Searle & Associates LLC and at its website www.anniesearle.com [February 2012-June 2013]

USA Library of Congress Control Number: 2012931422

ISBN # 978-0-9839347-6-9

Cover design by Jesse Brown

Contents

Acknowledgements

Not every businessperson employs and mentors students, sharing professional experience and wisdom. Not every teacher works to both impart knowledge and publish his or her students' work.

Annie Searle exemplifies what it means to be a teacher and businesswoman who goes above and beyond the norm to support, encourage, and challenge her students and associates alike.

She provided an invaluable experience when she hired me as a research associate during my graduate studies, and I most certainly would not be where I am today without her influence.

All of us connected with this publication – both research associates and students – have without a doubt benefited in many large and small ways from our connection with her.

Thanks, Annie.

Emily Oxenford, Editor
Former ASA Research Associate, 2010-2011

Forward

It is no small matter that we have a second, larger volume of research notes to offer less than two years after the first volume of Reflections on Risk appeared in 2012. ASA's research associate for any given academic year produces nine such notes, and I thank both Andrew Hansen (2011-2012) and Devin Luco (2012-2013) for their contributions. You will find also in this volume a research note from Divya Yadav (2013-2014), written before she takes up that research associate role this fall. We honor the internship program between ASA and the University of Washington's Information School, which spans five years.

The other research notes in this volume come from my work as a part-time faculty member in the Information School, where I started teaching in the spring of 2012. My courses are a mix of theory and real world examples. They focus strongly on the ability to speak and write about complex issues in such a way that executives can understand levels of urgency and next steps. My students use a research lens to examine the key operational risk issues facing both our government and the private sector. The research notes you will read were originally papers submitted through one of the courses I teach – an introductory and an advanced operational risk course, as well as a core course on the effects of information and technology on the study of ethics, policy and law. They were edited into research notes and published first in ASA News & Notes, our monthly newsletter, then made available on our website. The bar against which they can be measured is very high: they represent the issues of our time in an intelligible manner, and often make cutting edge recommendations for managing the risks as well.

All 26 research notes have gone through additional scrutiny to be published in this volume. I am grateful to Emily Oxenford, former ASA research associate (2010-2011), for taking on this project in her spare time. She is especially qualified to have edited the volume, since she wrote nine of the research notes in the first volume. Part of her job with this volume is to organize the notes into proper topic areas and to write an abstract note for each of them as well.

As I noted in the first volume, our research has been informed from the outset by my affiliation with New York University's Global Risk Forum, which continues to provide an inflection point for perspectives from both the private and public sectors on our most urgent threats.

Finally, this second volume is proof of what I have said for years, but which is especially true when you teach: you always get back more than you give.

Annie Searle
Seattle, Washington
November 2013

The Contributors

Daniel Arnaudo is currently a FLAS Senior Research Fellow at the University of Washington pursuing a Master of Arts degree in International Studies with a regional focus on Brazil and a topical focus on information and cybersecurity policy. He has a Master of Science degree in Information Management from the University of Washington and a Bachelor of Arts in International Studies from Emory University. His main research focus is to build a model of the interactions between the various actors and institutions that coordinate Brazilian Internet governance and infrastructure. In the past, he has covered national security, arms control and nuclear nonproliferation issues for a number of NGOs, including the Arms Control Association, the Center on International Cooperation and the Carter Center while building and maintaining their information resources.

Swati Chaturvedi received her Bachelor of Engineering degree from Rajiv Gandhi Proudyogiki Vishwavidyalaya, majoring in Electronics & Communications. She has five years of experience in software development and management working in India, the United Kingdom, and the U.S. in the telecommunication and insurance industries. She received her Master of Science in Information

Management (MSIM) in 2013, and then joined KPMG's risk consulting practice this past summer.

Andrew H. R. Hansen joined ASA as a research associate for the 2011-2012 academic year. He compiled the 22 research notes that are part of the first volume of Reflections on Risk (2012). He holds a Bachelor of Science degree in Information Systems from the University of Utah, and received his Master of Science in Information Management from the University of Washington's School of Information in 2012. He is a skilled researcher with prior experience at Boeing, H-11 Digital Forensics, and the State of Utah. He is currently working as a product manager, conducting research, writing, and data analysis for Seattle-based Reviews.com.

Delbert Hazeley is an information science professional, currently providing technology solutions in the public safety industry in an IT management position with the University of Washington Police. Previous professional pursuits include positions in the insurance industry, as a system administrator for a national title & escrow company based in the U.S., and before that working in the higher education industry as an IT intern for a public university. Del recently completed his Master of Science degree in Information Management at the University of Washington's Information School in

2013. He holds a Bachelor of Science degree in Information Science and Technology from the Pennsylvania State University, obtained in 2008.

Abbas Khambati received his Bachelor of Science degree in Engineering from the University of Mumbai and worked for two years at IGATE Corporation as a software engineer after graduation. He received his Master of Science in Information Management from the University of Washington's Information School in 2013. His recent work experience includes an internship at the Microsoft Global Security Operation Center where he focused on operational risk-related technology initiatives for Microsoft. He since has accepted a position as a consultant at Ernst & Young in the IT Risk Assurance practice.

Ilya Krivulin holds a Bachelor of Arts degree in Computer Science and a Bachelor of Arts degree in Mathematics, both from Jamestown College, and a Master of Science in Information Management from the University of Washington at Seattle. His experience includes positions as an implementation consultant at Fast Enterprises, LLC and as a technical consultant at F5 Networks, Inc. His current position is as engineer/consultant at Edgile, Inc.

Devin Luco joined ASA Risk Consultants as a research associate for the 2012-2013 academic year.

He received his Bachelor of Arts degree in Business Administration from the University of Washington's Foster School of Business, with an emphasis on accounting and finance. He is currently enrolled in the Master of Science in Information Management degree program at the UW Information School. His prior experience includes the financial planning group of The Boeing Company, where he was a financial analyst; and a 2013 summer internship at KPMG in the risk consulting advisory practice.

Jess Mauer received her Bachelor of Science degree in psychology from the University of Oregon with a minor in business. She then discovered a love of technology after accidentally acquiring a job with Apple. After tinkering around with computers for a few years and some travel, she returned to school and received a Master of Science in Information Management (MSIM) with a specialization in information security in 2013. She currently works in IT for Boeing.

Suzann Parker received her Bachelor of Arts degree in art education from Colorado State University. Her expertise is in technology project management and strategic information management in the non-profit sector. She has worked with nonprofits of all types and sizes to successfully implement business solutions for over ten years as a systems consultant, project manager, and portfolio/program manager. She is currently the Client Portfolio Manager at Beyond Nines and has just completed her Master of Science in Information Management at the University of Washington.

Chitra Raman received her Bachelor of Engineering from Goa University majoring in Computer Science. She is currently enrolled in the Master of Science in Information Management program at the University of Washington's Information School. Her prior experience includes working with JD Edward's ERP Group in Oracle where she was an applications engineer responsible for stakeholder communication management, system research and application development. Currently she is working with HomeAway as a software engineering intern.

Rashmi Shekhar received her Bachelor of Engineering degree from Visvesvaraya Technological University, majoring in Information Science. She has since worked as a software engineer and participated in academic projects and research activities. Her interests include strategic analysis, business case development, and prototyping. She will receive her Master of Science in Information Management in 2014. She is currently interning at Disney Worldwide Services.

Rajesh Subramanian is a graduate of the University of Mumbai, with an undergraduate degree in Computer Science. He received his Master of Science in Information Management from the Information School at University of Washington in 2013. After having interned with KPMG LLP in their Information Protection and Business Resilience services while he was finishing his degree, he has accepted a full time position with KPMG LLP.

Travis J. Warren received his Bachelor of Science in Information Technology from the University of Phoenix while working as a lead software analyst for Boeing. He recently graduated from the University of Washington with a Master of Science in Information Management degree and continues to work at Boeing, currently as a technical architect for numerous highly visible, customer-facing software systems.

Divya Yadav received her Bachelor of Science in Electronics and Communications from UP Technical University, India. She worked for three years as a software developer with multinational corporations like Mahindra Satyam and HCL Technologies in India. She is currently pursuing her Master of Science in Information Management from University of Washington. Divya will be the ASA research associate during the 2013-2014 academic year. Her interests lie with risk management, information architecture and program management.

Emily Oxenford received her Bachelor of Arts in International Studies from American University in Washington D.C., with a focus on Peace and Conflict Resolution. She attained her Master of Science in Information Management degree from the University of Washington's Information School in 2011, and from 2010-2011 served as ASA's research associate. She is a contributing author to the first volume of Reflections on Risk published in 2012 by the ASA Institute for Risk and Innovation. Emily currently works as a research analyst for Moss Adams LLP, a Seattle-based accounting and consulting firm, performing a wide variety of financial and business research services.

Chapter I
Critical Infrastructure

Protecting Critical Infrastructure

Andrew H. R. Hansen

June 2012

Abstract – *Advances in technology have made critical infrastructures more efficient, but have also introduced new threats. Andrew discusses how the Sentient Hyper-Optimized Data Access Network ("Shodan") exposes potential weaknesses by identifying Internet facing industrial control system devices. After providing an overview of smart grids, which have the capability to provide more efficient energy consumption, Andrew notes some of the existing threats that have security experts concerned. Andrew cautions that risk managers should assess the ways potential compromises to critical infrastructure could impact organizations and take appropriate measures to mitigate identified threats.*

Introduction

The critical infrastructures of the U.S. have developed a highly complex and co-dependent relationship. Protecting and ensuring the continuity of these critical infrastructures is "essential to the nation's security, public health and safety, economic vitality, and way of life."[1] The rapid technological advances of the previous two decades have resulted in improved efficiency and increased performance of several critical infrastructure sectors, but weaknesses in these systems are "among the country's greatest threats to national security."[2] This research note will introduce the critical infrastructure sectors, discuss an emerging hacking resource, analyze specific challenges facing the smart grid, and conclude with recommendations organizations can take to help ensure their systems are protected.

Critical Infrastructure

Critical infrastructure are the "assets, systems, and networks, whether physical or virtual, so vital to the U.S. that their incapacitation or destruction would have a debilitating effect on security, national economic security, public health or safety, or any combination thereof."[3] The Homeland Security Presidential Directive 7 established U.S. policy for enhancing critical infrastructure protection, and "for each sector, designated a federal Sector-Specific Agency (SSA) to lead protection and resilience-building programs and activities."[4] Through this directive and other legislative efforts spanning more than a decade, the following eighteen[5] infrastructure sectors have been identified as critical:

- Food & Agriculture
- Commercial Facilities
- Postal & Shipping

- Defense & Industrial Base
- Information Technology
- Banking & Finance
- Dams
- Communications
- Energy
- Government Facilities
- Critical Manufacturing
- Emergency Services
- Healthcare & Public Health
- Nuclear Reactors, Materials & Waste
- National Monuments & Icons
- Chemical
- Water
- Transportation Systems

Protection of these infrastructures has been deemed especially important as attacks "could significantly disrupt the functioning of government and business alike and produce cascading effects far beyond the targeted sector and physical location of the incident."[6] Many of these sectors are governed by industrial control systems, which is a high-level term that encompasses "supervisory control and data acquisition (SCADA) systems, distributed control systems (DCS), and other control system configuration such as skid-mounted Programmable Logic Controllers (PLC)."[7]

Industrial control systems were initially isolated systems, running specialized proprietary hardware and software.[8] However, recent years has seen widely available, low-cost Internet Protocol (IP) devices replacing these proprietary solutions. Because industries like electric, water and wastewater, oil and natural gas, transportation, chemical and many others typically utilize industrial control systems, this shift away from proprietary technology to common IP technology could increase the possibility of cyber security vulnerabilities and incidents.[9]

Shodan

Sentient Hyper-Optimized Data Access Network, or Shodan, has been referred to as the Google for hackers, and is "essentially a search engine for servers, routers, load balances, and computers."[10] The database developed by Shodan was built by indexing metadata in the headers contained in the hardware broadcasts to other devices.[11] Shodan provides the ability to find devices based on "city, country, latitude/longitude, hostname, operating system, and IP,"[12] which means that, "not only can it identify a Solaris server, it can in many cases identify a Solaris server located in Pakistan that remains vulnerable to a known exploit."[13] With a tool like Shodan, the resources necessary to locate and identify Internet-facing SCADA systems has been greatly reduced, a concerning fact that has not escaped the attention of security experts.

In October 2010, following several reports from multiple independent security researchers, the Industrial Control Systems Cyber Emergency

Response Team (ICS-CERT) issued an alert specifically addressing Shodan's ability to expose control system vulnerabilities. The ICS-CERT alert identified systems spanning several critical infrastructures, specifically mentioning the increased risk of account brute force attacks as some of the systems "continue to use default user names and passwords and/or common vendor accounts for remote access to these systems."[14] More alarming, many of these default credentials can easily be found online.[15] As discussed in a previous research note on trends in security breaches, the Stuxnet worm that reportedly burrowed into SCADA systems controlling Iranian nuclear power plants is a good example of the kinds of infrastructure attacks a resource like Shodan can help facilitate.

Although the compromising of any of the critical infrastructures would result in cascading and far reaching consequences, according to former CIA Director John Woosley, "One of (the greatest threats) is the vulnerability of our electricity grid to hackers and to physical attack on things like transformers... All of the 17 other (critical infrastructures) depend on the electrical grid."[16] The following section will discuss some of the challenging security issues facing the electrical grid as it transitions to a "smart grid."

Smart Grid

The term "smart grid" refers to the computerization of the existing power grid and adds "monitoring, analysis, control, and communication capabilities to the national electrical delivery system to maximize the throughput of the system while reducing the energy consumption."[17] The two-way digital devices aim to empower utilities to maximize efficiency by better controlling power distribution and allowing homeowners and businesses to use electricity as economically as possible.[18] With $3.4 billion in stimulus funds being injected into smart grid technologies, an estimated 60 million American households and businesses are projected to deploy the technology in 2012 alone.[19] This will very likely result in more efficient energy consumption, but with "multiple credible threats" to the smart grid already in existence, many security experts feel the transition is premature.[20]

According to security experts, some of the meters and other points on the smart grid are susceptible to existing forms of attacks. In fact, professional security firm IOActive determined "that an attacker with $500 of equipment and materials and a background in electronics and software engineering could 'take command and control of the [advanced meter infrastructure] allowing for the en masse

manipulation of service to homes and businesses.'"
Once a hacker was in the system, they could
potentially "gain control of thousands, even millions,
of meters and shut them off simultaneously."[21] In
addition, a hacker could also be able to dramatically
alter the demand for power, disrupting the load
balance on the local power grid, and result in a
blackout.[22]

Extended loss of power can have enormous
consequences on the economy. On August 14, 2003 a
power surge affected the transmission grid resulting
in a blackout along the border of the U.S. and Canada
leaving more than 50 million people without power.[23]
The majority of areas impacted had power fully
restored within two days, but part of Ontario
experienced rolling blackouts for more than a week.[24]
Most figures estimate the cost of the blackout to be
around $6 billion, including costs like lost income to
workers, extra costs to government agencies (due to
overtime and emergency service costs), costs
associated with lost or spoiled commodities, and costs
associated with other industry specific losses (i.e.
delays in shipping impacting supply chains).[25]

Since the 2003 blackout, the utility industry has made
great improvements to its ability to detect and isolate
outages and is projecting that some elements of new
smart grid technology will enhance that capability.[26]

Representatives from the industry seem to be aware of the potential problems, and say they do not intend to install an unsafe grid online.[27] But as the smart grid continues to develop, risk managers should exercise caution and ensure potential threats have been appropriately remedied.

Recommendations

In terms of responding to Shodan and other resources like it, the ICS-CERT alert recommended the following[28] actions:

- Placing all control systems assets behind firewalls, separated from the business network
- Deploying secure remote access methods such as Virtual Private Networks (VPNs) for remote access
- Removing, disabling, or renaming any default system accounts (where possible)
- Implementing account lockout policies to reduce the risk from brute forcing attempts
- Implementing policies requiring the use of strong passwords
- Monitoring the creation of administrator level accounts by third-party vendors

ICS-CERT also recommended control system owners and operators to audit their control systems for the use of default administrator level user names and passwords – regardless of whether or not the system is connected to the Internet.[29] Risk managers should constantly be researching tools like Shodan, and if appropriate, using the services to identify weaknesses in their own systems.

Risk managers should also ensure that disaster recovery and business continuity plans specifically address responding to a loss of power. Should an organization ever lose access to power from the grid, alternative power sources such as generators can ensure critical systems and functions can continue to operate as expected without interruption. Servicing the standby generators and conducting regular tests will further enable an organization to respond effectively should a man-made or natural disaster strike. Installing surge protectors, protective software, and backing up data are all additional ways organizations can protect their systems and ensure damage from lost data and productivity is kept to a minimum.

Conclusion

At a recent cyber security conference, Director of the Federal Bureau of Investigation (FBI) Robert S. Mueller, said, "Terrorism remains the FBI's top priority. But in the not too distant future, we anticipate that the cyber threat will pose the number one threat to our country."[30] As critical infrastructures continue to be influenced by advances in technology, opportunities for exploitation will also rise. It is clear that even basic compromises to critical infrastructures would have far-reaching, detrimental consequences. Risk managers should constantly be mindful of the ways new devices can introduce new risk, and be confident in the security features before introducing the device into work processes.

This research note intended to specifically bring to light potential concerns challenging energy – a critical infrastructure that if compromised will affect every other sector. As the threat of state sponsored attacks increases, risk managers should take the time to research the other critical infrastructures, and understand how compromises in each infrastructure could potentially impact their organization and prepare and implement appropriate remediation plans.

---

[1] "Critical Infrastructure." U.S. Department of Homeland Security. n. d. Accessed 5 Jun. 2012 <www.dhs.gov>.

[2] Ferran, Lee and Jason Ryan. "DHS Deploys Special Teams to Battle Hackers in Cyber War for Infrastructure." *ABC News.* 4 Aug. 2010. Accessed 5 Jun. 2012 <www.theintelshop.com>

[3] Critical Infrastructure.

[4] Ibid.

[5] Ibid.

[6] Ibid.

[7] Falco, Joe, Karen Scarfone, and Keith Stouffer. "Guide to Industrial Control Systems (ICS) Security." National Institute of Standards and Technology. Jun. 2011. Accessed 6 Jun. 2012 <www.csrc.nist.gov>

[8] Ibid.

[9] Ibid.

[10] Naraine, Ryan. "Shodan Search Exposes Insecure SCADA Systems." *Zdnet.* 2 Nov. 2010. Accessed 6 Jun. 2012 <www.zdnet.com>.

[11] Goodin, Dan. "Hackers Tap SCADA Vuln Search Engine." *The Register.* 2 Nov. 2010. Accessed 6 Jun. 2012 <www.theregister.co.uk>.

[12] "Shodan Finds Computers." *Shodan.com.* n. pg. Accessed 6 Jun. 2012 <www.shodanhq.com>

[13] Goodin.

[14] "Industrial Control Systems Cyber Emergency Response Team." U.S. Computer Emergency Readiness Team, U.S. Department of Homeland Security. n. d. Accessed 6 Jun. 2012 <www.us-cert.gov>.

[15] Ibid.

[16] Ferran.

[17] "What is Smart Grid and Why is it Important." National Electrical Manufacturers Association. n. d. Accessed 6 Jun. 2012 <www.nema.org>.

[18] Ibid.

[19] Barak, Sylvie. "National Security Threat: Hacking the Smart Grid." *EDN.com* 5 Apr. 2012. Accessed 6 Jun. 2012 <www.edn.com>.

[20] Ibid.

[21] Meserve, Jeanne. "'Smart Grid' May be Vulnerable to Hackers." *CNN Tech.* 20 Mar. 2009. Accessed 7 Jun. 2012 <www.articles.cnn.com>.

[22] Ibid.

[23] "The Economic Impacts of the Aug. 2003 Blackout." Electronic Consumers Resource Council. 9 Feb. 2004. Accessed 7 Jun. 2012 <www.elcon.org>.

[24] The Economic Impacts.

[25] The Economic Impacts.

[26] Meserve.

[27] Ibid.

[28] Goodin.

[29] "ICS-CERT Alert." U.S. Computer Emergency Readiness Team, U.S.
      Department of Homeland Security. 28 Oct. 2010. Accessed 7 Jun.
      2012 <www.us-cert.gov>.

[30] *Speeches: RSA Cyber Security Conference, San Francisco, CA*. Federal Bureau of
      Investigation, U.S. Department of Justice. 1 Mar. 2012. Accessed 7
      Jun. 2012 <www.fbi.gov>.

Risk and the Communications Sector

Swati Chaturvedi
July 2012

Abstract: *The communications sector is a key component in both the public and private sectors. Swati provides an overview of the relationships between the communication sector and government and private companies. She highlights how technology advancements have created new risks for the communications sector, demanding the attention of both government and private companies for managing and reducing risks. The research note presents recommendations for ensuring that the country's communications networks and systems are secure and resilient in the face of these new risks.*

Introduction

This research note discusses the key risks, hazards, and vulnerabilities related to the communications sector in both the public and private sectors. Further, this research note reviews the role of government agencies in regulating the communications sector, their effectiveness in exercising sector-specific controls and their relationship with the private sector in coordinating efforts to reduce risk across the communications sector. This research note also examines the interdependencies between the communications sector and other critical infrastructures. Lastly, recommendations are presented for improving and enhancing the protection and resiliency of both sectors.

Overview

Communications is one of the eighteen critical infrastructures and key resources (CIKR) sector of the U.S. that is essential to the national security, public health and safety, economic prosperity and operations of government and all businesses.[1] The communications sector - consisting of wired, wireless, satellite, cable, broadcasting, and Internet - forms the communications backbone of the U.S. economy, and is vital to a wide range of industries in both the public and private sectors.

The majority of operators in the communications sector in the U.S. are privately owned. The Federal Communications Commission (FCC) serves as the governmental oversight agency and the U.S. Department of Homeland Security's (DHS) National Communications Center (NCC)[2] serves as the designated Sector Specific Agency. As the communications sector governing agency, the FCC is responsible for designing policy frameworks, supporting emergency operations, ensuring public safety, universal availability and accessibility of basic telecommunications service to everyone and protecting interests of the consumer in the communications marketplace. The NCC, on the other hand, works in collaboration with its partners to develop and implement the Communications Sector Specific Plan (CSSP)[3] for reducing risks across the communications sector and improving the protection and resilience-building programs and activities. The CSSP lays out the coordinated protection strategy allowing the federal government to develop and execute plans for national security and public safety, while permitting private companies to reduce operational risks, maintain business continuity, and achieve the sector goals by utilizing resources from both the public and private sectors.

Risks – Government Side

The FCC faces a variety of risks from both the internal and external threats. Some of these risks include malware attacks, malicious email links, phishing, cyber criminals, hackers, insider threat, hactivists, and terrorist attacks.[4]

Cyber-attacks and security breach incidents against government agencies such as U.S. Senate, Central Intelligence Agency (CIA), InfraGard, and Arizona Department of Public Safety in the past years emphasize the risk of cyber-attacks from cyber criminals and hackers through means of malware, malicious email links, phishing etc. for the FCC and its critical information systems.[5]

Just like any other organization, the FCC runs the risk of insider threats from disgruntled employees and unauthorized staff access, which could lead to misuse of critical information, intentional misappropriation of the FCC assets, and misuse of individual position or authority in the government agency to commit insider fraud.

The FCC also faces the risk of hactivism, where its computer networks could be misused to protest political ends or promote political ideology by spamming political ideals and issues. These activities could disrupt national peace and lead to political upheaval in the country or certain sections of society.

The importance of the communications sector to national safety, economic prosperity, and public wellness makes government agencies like the FCC and its partners potential targets of terrorist groups. Any terrorist attack on the FCC or its partners could directly influence the effectiveness of emergency 911 calls, national emergency alert systems, and radio and television broadcast stations for news and updates that are vital to achieving a successful response to emergency operations.

Risks – Private Sector Side

Some of the risks described above are also relevant to the private sector, and some risks are specific to the private sector. Private-sector risks primarily include threats to services provided by a company. This research note will discuss risks for two private entities in the sector – Comcast[6] and Sprint[7], though identified risks can be extended to other companies in the communications sector as well. Some of the risks relevant to these companies are:

- Technological advancements
- Loss of intellectual property
- Security breach and cyber-attacks on the communications network
- Blurring dividing lines between the various communication services
- Market competition and consolidation
- Weak economic conditions
- Regulatory restrictions and additional costs

Most private sector companies in the communications sector face the threats associated with technological advancements such as IP technology, 4G technologies, due to the rapid pace of market-changing advancements in digital technology. Changes in technology may cause uncertainty regarding future subscriber demands for the communication services, service pricing, and ability of service providers to meet the technology advancements on a timely basis. Failure to effectively respond to these technology advancements can seriously affect the company's operations and business.

Companies in the communications industry rely heavily on the use of intellectual property such as patents, copyrights, and trademarks owned internally or through third party and vendors. Legal challenges or claims regarding infringement of intellectual property can incur substantial liability in terms of time, money and resources affecting not only a company's reputation in the market but also limiting its ability to compete effectively in the marketplace.

Security breaches of information systems could lead to misuse or loss of company data, customer information, and vendor relations. Additionally, the increased threat from cyber-attacks, hacking, and denial of service attacks on the network can have both a devastating effect on company's reputation and financial standing. Attacks could also seriously affect national security and public safety. A few examples of cyber-attacks and security breach incidents on private companies in the communications sector in recent times are Fox Broadcasting Company, PBS, and L3 Communications.

Joint ventures and recent advancements in the communications sector has blurred the traditional line among the communication services such as long distance, local, wireless, video, internet and satellite by integrating these services into packages. These changing trends can influence the pricing models of the communication services affecting the company's financial strength, revenues, growth, and profitability.

Mergers and acquisitions in the communications sector have consolidated the communications marketplace allowing few players to exercise increased control in the market and hence disrupting the balance in the national Communications ecosystem.

Weak economic conditions in the U.S. and global economy impacts customer discretionary spending patterns, and may reduce the number of consumers willing or able to subscribe to certain discretionary services such as cable TV, high-speed Internet connections, and large data plans for mobile devices.

Regulations from government agencies may increase operating costs and restrict what services operators in the communications sector can offer to customers. Failure to comply with regulations carries a further risk of penalties, fines, license revocation, and other liabilities that could adversely affect the business operations and market reputation for the companies in the private sector.

Controls

Some of the risks mentioned in this research note can be dealt with internally by company specific controls. Others require sector-specific controls and are dependent on policies and regulations by the FCC, the Sector Specific Agency NCC, and their partners. In order to mitigate risks, the FCC has laid out certain regulations to govern the communications sector.[8]

Currently, the FCC requires wireless and broadcasting infrastructure owners to file information on the communications equipment location and type. The FCC mandates wire line, wireless, cable, and satellite carriers and operators to annually submit data on infrastructure, network outages, and financial standing allowing the FCC to measure competition and service quality. Furthermore, the FCC maintains a team of experts to analyze this data in an attempt to reveal troublesome trends in network reliability and security, assess cause of network outages, and evaluate measures used to restore service. Analysis of this data lets the FCC determine the adoption of best practices and devise revisions to further improve the communications network reliability and security across the sector.

Apart from this, the FCC is also responsible for allocating spectrum for public safety[9] and television broadcasting; commercial licensing of radio waves; the regulation of obscenity, indecency, and profanity of broadcast content; and maintaining fair market practices and sound competition to protect consumer interests in the communications sector.

This section discusses few examples to demonstrate FCC regulations in action and determine their effectiveness. A recent example of this is the failure of AT&T and T-Mobile merger.[10] The FCC determined that approval of the merger of the two wireless operator giants would drastically reduce market competition. The FCC believed the merger would hamper investment in the wireless space, and questioned the underlying claims of serving public interest and necessity. Based on their investigation and above considerations, the FCC ruled against the merger of AT&T and T-Mobile securing consumer interest in the communications marketplace.

This however is not always the case. According to another recent example, the consumer watchdogs at the Environmental Working Group accused the FCC of deliberately shielding information from the public about possible concerns related to cell phone radiation in response to pressure from the Cellular Telecommunications and Internet Association

(CTIA).[11] The FCC however, responded to these claims by saying that there is "no scientific evidence that proves that wireless phone usage can lead to cancer."[12] As a body responsible for regulating cell phones and the communications sector, the FCC should address consumer concerns, provide relevant references related to the subject matter, and appropriately advise consumers on potential risks and suggestions for mitigation.

Interdependencies

Other critical infrastructures depend heavily on the communications sector, which shares interdependency with the energy, information technology, financial, postal operations, and emergency services sectors.[13] Both the government agencies and private sector companies in the communications sector rely heavily on the energy sector for power to run the cellular towers, central offices and other critical communication facilities and infrastructure. Information technologies such as control systems, software, and operating systems provide critical services. The financial sector relies on telecommunications for the transmission of financial transactions and stock market operations. The postal and shipping sector relies on the communications sector for tracking shipments and running control systems. Lastly, emergency services depend on the telecommunications for receiving emergency 911 calls and accordingly disseminating resources, coordinating responses, alerting the public, and facilitating the responses to emergencies. These interdependencies highlight the importance of the communications sector not only for direct customers but also for supporting the smooth operation of other critical infrastructure sectors.

Recommendations

The pattern of rapid transformations in the communications sector requires regular reviews of government regulations and the implementation and adoption of regulations in the private sector. Key recommendations for the public sector for next steps include:

- Keep pace with technology advancements - review, create, and update regulations and policies to maintain relevancy
- Develop and implement agile, effective, cost efficient and robust cyber security approaches to deal with the growing threat of cyber-attacks and security breaches
- Enhance public safety infrastructure and emergency call service to enable the transmission of text, image, and video with the introduction of the Next-Gen 911[14] system

- Distribute information on public interest issues such as relevant research, usage recommendations, and education material on consumer rights

While it is important that the FCC implements the above recommendations, it is equally vital that as a Sector Specific Agency, the NCC updates the Communications Sector Specific Plan (CSSP). The NCC improves collaboration with its partners to include appropriate measures and controls to reduce operational risks and improve protections and resilience-building programs and activities. These controls prove to be more effective in reducing risk across the communications sector if implemented industry-wide, leveraging resources from both the public and private sectors. Based on this premise, the key recommendations for managing risk and maintaining business continuity in the private sector side are:

- Maintain pace with technology advances to offer competitive services and prices
- Develop and implement agile, effective, cost efficient and robust cyber security approaches to deal with the growing threat of cyber-attacks and security breaches

- Ensure compliance to changing regulations by increasing frequency of internal control audits
- Protect intellectual property such as copyrights, trademarks etc. and avoid infringements by increasing awareness amongst employees and partners regarding effective management and use of intellectual property

In addition to the above recommendations, it is highly advised that efforts be made to improve collaboration and partnership between the FCC, the NCC, state and local governments, and private sector companies to effectively manage risk and maintain a healthy ecosystem in the communications sector.

---

[1] *National Infrastructure Protection Plan - Communications Sector.* U.S. Department of Homeland Security. Aug. 2011. Accessed 5 Jun. 2012 <www.dhs.gov>.

[2] "Communications Sector." U.S. Department of Homeland Security. n.d. Accessed 5 Jun. 2012 <www.dhs.gov>.

[3] *Communications Sector-Specific Plan.* U.S. Department of Homeland Security. 2010. Accessed 5 Jun. 2012 <www.dhs.gov>.

[4] Ibid.

[5] "Cyber Security Executive Update." National Institute of Standards and Technology, U.S. Department of Commerce. 25 Jul. 2011. Accessed 5 Jun. 2012 <www.csrc.nist.gov>.

[6] *2011 Annual Report on Form 10-K.* Comcast Corporation. 22 Feb. 2011. Accessed 6 Jun. 2012 <www.comcast.com>.

[7] *Section 1: 10-K (Form 10-K).* Sprint Nextel Corporation. Feb. 2012. Accessed 6 Jun. 2012 <www.investors.sprint.com>

[8] *Communications Sector-Specific Plan.*

[9] Moore, Linda K. "CRS Report for Congress." 23 Jun. 2005. Accessed 6 Jun. 2012
        <www.au.af.mil>

[10] Velazco, Chris. "The AT&T/T-Mobile Merger Is Dead." *TechCrunch.* , 19 Dec.
        2011. Accessed 6 Jun. 2012 <www.techcrunch.com>

[11] Sheppard, Kate. "Is the FCC Downplaying Potential Risks from Cell Phone
        Radiation?"*MotherJones.* 3 Jun. 2011. Accessed 6 Jun. 2012
        <www.motherjones.com>

[12] Ibid.

[13] "Communications Sector: Critical Infrastructure." U.S. Department of
        Homeland Security. n.d. Accessed 5 Jun. 2012 <www.dhs.gov>.

[14] Jackson, William . "FCC's 5-step plan for deploying Next-Gen
        911." *Government Computer News (GCN).* 8 May 2012. Accessed 6
        Jun. 2012 <www.gcn.com>

Risk and the Water Sector

Ilya Krivulin
September 2012

Abstract – *Ilya provides an overview of the importance of the water utility sector, the important role it plays in society, and highlights some of the key players responsible for governing the sector. The research note identifies potential operational risks associated with the sector, the impact those risks create, provides real life examples of operational breaches, and explains why this particular sector is just so important.*

Introduction

The Homeland Security Presidential Directive-7 (HSPD) has identified eighteen critical infrastructure and key resources (CIKR) sectors that are critical in maintaining the country's infrastructure in terms of day-to-day operations, viability, and economic sustainability. The Directive describes ways to protect these sectors from terrorist attacks and other hazards in sector- (and context) specific plans in support of the risk management framework called National Infrastructure Protection Plan (NIPP). This research note will focus on the water sector. It will identify the sector "assets" and the potential operational risks associated with those assets on the government side, extend the discussion about risks and vulnerabilities into the private sector, provide real-life examples of operational breach and conclude with a few recommendations for further mitigation of the risks discussed.

Why the Water Sector?

Historically, water has been an integral part of human existence: simply put, humans physically cannot survive without an uninterrupted supply of clean drinking water. The proper treatment and disposal of wastewater is also critical in the prevention of disease and contamination. Both of these types of water – drinking and wastewater – comprise the water sector.

"There are approximately 160,000 public drinking water systems and more than 16,000 publicly owned wastewater treatment systems in the U.S. Approximately 84 percent of the U.S. population receives their potable water from these drinking water systems and more than 75 percent of the U.S. population has its sanitary sewerage treated by these wastewater systems."[1]

Alongside individual consumption, important organizations such as hospitals, educational facilities (i.e. schools and universities), airports, stadiums and arenas, large event venues, firefighting equipment (like fire hydrants) are all highly dependent on an uncontaminated water supply and proper disposal. In addition to this, research shows that the water sector, despite having a rich history of water quality monitoring under the guidance of the Safe Water Drinking Act (SDWA) and the Clean Water Act (CWA),[2] was not developed with security in mind, particularly in comparison to the energy and nuclear sectors, for instance.[3]

If all communication and contact with the rest of the world was cut out off by a major disaster, people could spend many nights in darkness and cold because of power outages; without food, people could survive for quite a few days; but without water people generally do not survive even 48 hours.

Who Is in Charge?

The HSPD-7 has designated the U.S. Environmental Protection Agency (EPA) as the government body responsible for establishing various programs that support security-related activities, "With the goal of enhancing the water sector's ability to plan for and respond effectively to security threats and breaches."[4] It is important to note here that the NIPP relies on partnerships and extensive communication between the members to achieve the framework's goals of maintaining a secure and uninterruptable national infrastructure. Taken from a 2010 EPA report,[5] below is the summary of EPA's responsibilities and information about its partners.

EPA handles the receipt of community water systems vulnerability assessments (VAs) and emergency response plan (ERP) certifications.

The Water Security Initiative (WSI), the Active and Effective Security Program and the Water laboratory Alliance (WLA) programs work towards aiding the water sector in maintaining public health and protecting the environment.

The U.S. Department of Homeland Security (DHS) is a supervising partner in recognizing and reducing risks through risk assessments in the sector.

The Information Sharing and Analysis Center allows for gathering, analyzing, and disseminating threat information specific to the sector.

In order to enhance preparedness and response, Water/Wastewater Agency Response Networks (WARNs) are established.

In order to maintain a resilient infrastructure, a series of training exercises and drills in support of the National Incident Management Systems/Incident Command System (NIMS/ICS) are conducted to help water sector utilities have better communication and incident response.

EPA also collaborates with public and private utilities, national water sector associations, States, the Water Sector Coordinating Council, and the Government Coordinating Council to further enhance cooperation and security amongst water sector utilities.

What Is in the Systems?

Next, it is appropriate to introduce the components of water systems (this research note will focus on potable drinking water) and to identify sample assets and electronic systems in the water sector. The reason for enumerating these is that security breaches can happen to any of the components listed below, thus increasing EPA's range of responsibilities for mitigating risks. Depending on the size of the utility, the components may include all or some of the following[6]:

- Water Source (ground or surface)
- Conveyance – from a remote source to a treatment plant
- Raw water storage – reservoirs or lakes in remote or urban areas
- Treatment – physical and chemical, depending on contaminants detected in raw water
- Finished water storage – before distributing to customers;
- Distribution system

- Monitoring system – this one is of utmost importance as monitoring provides visibility into what needs change or upgrade in the controlling equipment as well as presents a potential security threat had the monitoring data, like the consistency of contaminants for example, leaked into malicious hands.
- Supervisory Control and Data Acquisition (SCADA) system – linkage (often wireless) between various components of the monitoring systems in order to provide necessary data or automate operations at a facility.

An "asset" in the water sector is defined to be "an entire system for purposes of identification, prioritization, and coordination."[7] Utilities are expected to run risk assessments of their own on each of the key components and assets that, if affected maliciously, will have negative effects on operations within and outside the sector. In addition to SCADA, the water sector information security infrastructure includes the following[8] assets:

- Central control station
- Human-machine interface
- Local processes, instruments and operating equipment

- Workforce – a lack of appropriately trained personnel may result in inability to carry out necessary operations and provide services to the customers.

Lastly, it is important to note that such databases as Safe Drinking Water Information System (SDWIS) contain very sensitive information, such as complete inventories of Public Water Systems, water sources, and detailed location and treatment information. Therefore, the data presents a potential security threat.

Risks and Impacts

As seen above, the potential risks in the water sector are vast and the occurrence of disaster may directly affect other sectors due to interconnectedness. The first and most obvious risk is the infection of public health due to agent contamination, release of poisonous gas, or any other malicious means of making water unusable. The extent of the impact would vary depending on how fast the problem is discovered and how dense the population is in the area of the incident. Since contamination can spread through more than just one way - like inhalation, ingestion, or skin absorption - the impact of drinking or otherwise consuming contaminated water is potentially huge.[9] It is important to keep in mind that a disease-stricken population means reduced workforce numbers, and therefore productivity may have a cascading diminishing effect on the economy. Closure of businesses, schools, and restaurants are all examples of an economic impact. Next comes the question about the infrastructure recovery: how long does it take to recover a broken utility and what happens when the systems inside that utility are customized and cannot be fixed by readily available equipment? Lastly, the psychological effect may be quite damaging. Even if the contamination does not result in many deaths, it may be quite arduous for a government to restore people's confidence, maintain order, and provide basic services while determining the cause of an incident and dealing with decontamination.[10]

Another very serious risk is cyber-attacks. Just like electrical power plants, water utilities are often controlled and monitored by some kind of computer system, or specifically a SCADA system as discussed above. An example of such a breach would be a recent attack on South Houston's water utility. The attack is believed to have come from Russia and the hacker obtained and publicly posted the screenshots of the utility control system that he claims to have gained access to in almost no time.[11] The hacker stated,

I dislike, immensely, how the DHS tend to downplay how absolutely (expletive deleted) the state of national

infrastructure is. I've also seen various people doubt the possibility of an attack like this could be done. So, y'know ... the city of South Houston has a really insecure system. Wanna see? I know ya do. I'm not going to expose the details of the box. No damage was done to any of the machinery; I don't really like mindless vandalism. It's stupid and silly. On the other hand, so is connecting interfaces to your SCADA machinery to the Internet. I wouldn't even call this a hack, either, just to say. This required almost no skill and could be reproduced by a two year old with a basic knowledge of Simatic."[12]

He brings up an interesting point of having the system connected to the external Internet. As long as an Ethernet switch accepts traffic from the outside, it creates an enormous potential for malicious intrusion and thus increases the amount of protection needed for such systems.

Another example comes from Los Angeles, where a local water utility decided to conduct a "pilot" study on the system's security potential. The water utility recruited a few volunteers to try to break the system (this testing technique is also used by companies in other sectors to test the security of systems). Afterwards, the utility reported that within two hours the testers had gained full control of the system without any insider guidance, and had they been malicious, they would been able to dump chemicals into LA River, making the water toxic, while turning off the sensors to detect the contamination.[13]

Some other common hazards include:[14]

- Improvised explosive devises
- Vehicle-born explosive devices
- Explosive devices in wastewater collection systems
- Radiological or biological contamination in drinking water distribution systems
- Assault
- Sabotage of water treatment systems

Additionally, the risks from natural disasters such as earthquakes and hurricanes cannot be overlooked.

Lastly, the importance of the interconnectedness of the water sector with other areas should be reiterated. For example, an occurrence of any of the above risks may halt operations of a power generation plant, since many rely on water flow for cooling. And vice versa - a water utility may come to a halt because of an interrupted power supply, since water utility control and operation systems are run, monitored, and controlled by electrical (computer) system.

Risk Assessment

Risks threats come from many different directions: whether it is a terrorist attack, a human mistake, or a computer malicious virus, water utilities need to be ready to respond in a timely manner. Next, a set of risk assessment initiatives and tools will be discussed, that the private sector currently undertakes and uses to reduce vulnerabilities and enhance preparedness.

As mentioned above, the EPA partners closely with the DHS to come up with risk assessment documents and tools in order to assist owners and operators in conducting local risk assessments and making sure that the methodologies are always up-to-date. The EPA has drafted numerous threat documents and holds workshops for raising awareness about various types of risks. The DHS also conducts SCADA educational workshops as part of their cyber security roadmap. The following three tools are the current main instruments of risk assessment in the water sector:[15]

- Risk Assessment Methodology – Water (RAM-W)
- Security and Environmental Management System (SEMS) emergency response checklist
- Vulnerability Self-Assessment Tool (VSAT)

Another example of government assistance to the private sector is the non-profit program called

LIGHTS. It is a programmatic solution that helps a number of smaller industries, including the water sector, establish the level of cyber security needed for current conditions. The solution expands visibility into systems, keeping it as cost effective as possible, and encourages participation from more communities around the country and even the world. It allows for sharing of anonymized metadata, "at member's discretion, to assist in efforts to increase the safety and reliability of our national infrastructure."[16] It also works with analysis centers to improve situational awareness.

There are many more examples of risk assessment initiatives. It also seems that the government has a good foundation for closely monitoring and mitigating risks associated with various critical sectors of the infrastructure, and has created documents and tools to support various initiatives. The government's responsibility to the private sector is outreach and education, since the local risk assessment is on the shoulders of the utilities. The threats, vulnerabilities, risks, and impact analysis is a complicated process that often requires professionals to carry out to make critical infrastructure safer. Educational institutions should encourage students interested in risk management to consider working for one of the sectors in government in addition to pursuing consulting in private firms.

Professional support helps organizations better understand the features and aspects of computer systems. During one of the cyber security breaches, the review discovered that the intrusion happened not because the system had some kind of vulnerability or a bug, but rather occurred because there were certain features enabled that the customer did not even know about.[17] Customers, i.e. utilities, should take responsibility in learning the systems that they purchase and vendors should be obliged to provide training upon demand.

Conclusion

This research note clearly showed the importance of the water sector to national interests. Vendors need to ensure they design the utility assets with security in mind. The CEO of Trusted Metrics, Michael Menefee, stated that if it were decided that the water sector was the most important critical infrastructure, then 12, 24, 36 months would not be enough to get everything done.[18] Both the government and private sectors need to continue to collaborate closely with each other in order to increase protection levels of our water supply facilities.

[1] "Water Sector Snapshot." U.S. Department of Homeland Security. 2009.
        Accessed 28 May 2012 <ww.dhs.gov>.

[2] *Water Sector-Specific Plan. An Annex to the National Infrastructure Protection
        Plan.* U.S. Department of Homeland Security. 2010. Accessed 1 Jun.
        2012 <www.dhs.gov>.

[3] Menefee, Michael. "Cybersecurity in Waste Water and Water Control
        Systems." *InfoSec Island.* 14 Dec. 2011. Accessed 2 Jun. 2012
        <www.infosecisland.com>

[4] *Water Sector-Specific Plan.*

[5] "Water Sector Snapshot."

[6] *Water Sector-Specific Plan.*

[7] *Water Sector-Specific Plan.*

[8] *Water Sector-Specific Plan.*

[9] *Water Sector-Specific Plan.*

[10] *Water Sector-Specific Plan.*

[11] Menefee.

[12] Byers, Eric. "SCADA Security Breached at U.S. Water Utilities." Tofino. 21
        Nov. 2011. Accessed 26 May 2012 <www.tofinosecurity.com >.

[13] Menefee.

[14] *Water Sector-Specific Plan.*

[15] *Water Sector-Specific Plan.*

[16] *LIGHTS.* Energy Sector Security Consortium, Inc. 2012. Accessed 27 May
        2012 <www.lights.energysec.org>.

[17] Menefee.

[18] Menefee.

Machine-to-Machine Communications

Devin Luco

February 2013

Abstract – *In this research note, Devin dives into the evolving world of machine-to-machine communications. After looking at some of the various ways the technology has been applied, and potential areas of growth, Devin discusses the benefits and associated risks the application of the technology can bring to organizations.*

Introduction

The concept of machine-to-machine (M2M) communications has been around for decades. In fact, the concept can be traced as far back as World War II, when pilots used identification, friend, or foe (IFF) to avoid hitting non-hostile targets.[1] Another technology, the remote controlled garage door, that may not be as old as IFF but something we all could probably relate to, which also uses the M2M communications concept.[2] However, being able to network the sensors in M2M devices, know that the garage door was left open, and send this information to the homeowner are new capabilities.[3] These types of interaction capabilities present in today's technology have given reasons to many industries and organizations to think of innovative ways to use M2M communication to improve productivity and efficiency. Pike Research reported in in 2008, only 4 percent of the world's 1.5 billion electric utility meters were considered "smart meters."[4] Four years later in 2012, an estimated 18 percent of total electric utility meters were classified as "smart."[5] The increase of smart meters - meters that use M2M communications - during this timeframe demonstrate that demand for the technology is on the rise. With the success of M2M technology in the utility industry, companies from other sectors are hoping to implement M2M in similar ways. However, it is not surprising that companies will need to be cautious before implementing M2M technologies, as there are associated risks that must be weighed against the possible benefits.

What is Machine-to-Machine Communication?

Machine-to-machine communications (M2M) is a term used to describe any wired or wireless automated communication between electronic machines.[6] The machines that are on this network can communicate and perform actions without human intervention.[7] An M2M system should have sensors, a Wi-Fi or cellular connection, and analytical software programs.[8] One of the factors that have caused the rise of M2M communications is that these components needed for an M2M system to work are becoming more accessible at lower costs with more power efficiency.[9] With the cost of the M2M components at a discount, the barriers to entry are no longer as high. Organizations are now more able to afford implementing M2M communications, which has led to increased interest from many industries.

To better picture how M2M works, imagine a utility company such as Puget Sound Energy. By installing M2M capable meters in homes or other establishments, utility companies are able to collect real-time usage data and automatically send data to central computers where it is analyzed, enabling billing to be determined without or with little manual assistance from humans. Other practical uses of M2M systems include remote diagnostic and failure prevention purposes for manufacturers of medical devices and heavy machinery.[10] The important part of M2M communications is not only that it can remotely monitor the status of the equipment, but it can also turn collected data into meaningful information such as triggering alerts for a manufacturer when a possible failure is on the horizon. This type of feature can help companies improve customer satisfaction and quality control.

The Benefits of M2M

Implementing M2M communications allows organizations to reap certain benefits including gathering data more efficiently, collecting data in larger quantities, and the flexibility of the sensor location.[11] As stated earlier, M2M can reduce the labor costs associated with collecting data manually, such as having to physically check and monitor the status of utility meters. Other potential cost savings include any training or transportation costs that are needed to conduct the manual job process. However, not only can M2M technologies reduce costs but it can also save a company time because a sensor can gather and send real-time data over a network much quicker than a technician collecting and reporting data. Additionally, M2M sensors can collect data constantly and in much larger quantities than a human can analyze or handle. With higher volumes of data at an organizations' disposal, utilizing the right tools and analyzing the large datasets it can lead to valuable information such as predicting industry trends (for more information on Big Data, please see the research note "What is Big Data?"). In addition, the sensors that collect data can communicate via a wireless or cellular network, which means the physical location of the sensor can be practically anywhere.[12] Although there are numerous benefits to using M2M communications, organizations must also ask what costs and risks are associated with implementation.

Risks of M2M Communications

As alluded to earlier, the implementation of machine-to-machine communications does not come without baggage. The most important risk factor of M2M is data security.[13] Whenever communication is taking place over a network, whether public or private, there is always a possibility of hackers interrupting the flow of data. For instance, using the earlier example of the garage door opener, imagine if someone hacked onto the network on which the M2M technology operates. A hacker could use the information about the garage door opening being sent over the network to track daily habits and schedules of the families that reside in that home. Last year at the Mobile World Conference in Barcelona, there were examples on display by AdaptiveMobile of how hackers can use mobile devices to walk right through your front door.[14] This is an example of just one security risk that comes with M2M technology. The invasion of privacy and loss of data many people have probably dealt with in the past due to hackers or malware attacks. However, with a hacker being able to physically enter a home or company building is a much scarier and harsher reality. Even more disturbing are potential hacks against medical devices, such as a heart monitor, which could lead to fatal attacks.[15] Another security risk involves the lack of human intervention. According to Cathal McDaid, security consultant at AdaptiveMobile, security vulnerabilities may be exploited for extended periods before someone actually notices and is able to correct the vulnerability.[16] The main point of having M2M communications is to reduce human interaction, which means the system may not be checked for longer periods of time. The longer a breach stays undetected, the greater the loss and negative impact an organization will realize. Another risk is the relative immaturity of the M2M communications technology in use today. Currently, the technology is still in the early stages of implementation, which means universal standards have not been established yet.[17] It may be in the best interest of an organization to wait until standards are established and approved before implementing M2M communications in order to avoid potential rework and restructuring.

Conclusion

Due to the lower component costs of machine-to-machine communications, the desire to create innovative ways for implementing M2M technologies has risen. Although implementing M2M can generate benefits in lower labor costs, reduction in failure rates, and discovering trends due to increased volumes of real-time data, like all new technologies it creates new risks and challenges. Challenges include the need to keep network security practices up to date and the existing lack of implementation standards. These challenges must be considered and addressed before an organization decides to implement M2M communications.

---

[1] Ruzicka, Nancee. "M2M Communications – Technology to Transform Business." *Forbes Custom*. Accessed 7 Feb. 2013. <www.forbescustom.com>

[2] Ibid.

[3] Ibid.

[4] Khan, Irfan. "Machine-to-Machine Communications Will Generate Really Big Data." *IT World*. 18 Oct. 2012. Accessed 8 Feb. 2013 <www.m.itworld.com>.

[5] Ibid.

[6] Rouse, Margaret. "Machine-to-Machine (M2M)." *WhatIs.com*. Jun. 2010. Accessed 7 Feb. 2013. <www.whatis.techtarget.com>.

[7] Ibid.

[8] Ibid.

[9] Ruzicka.

[10] Congdon, Ken. "What's M2M Mean To You?" *Field Technologies Online*. 23 Feb 2009. Accessed 7 Feb. 2013 <www.fieldtechnologiesonline.com>.

[11] Camden, Chip. "Consulting Opportunities and Potential Risks M2M Implementations." *Tech Republic*. 11 Jan. 2013. Accessed 7 Feb. 2013 <www.techrepublic.com>.

[12] Ibid.

[13] Ruzicka.

[14] "M2M Presents New Security Risks that Require New Security Solutions." *Info Security Magazine*. 28 Feb. 2012. Accessed 8 Feb. 2013 <www.infosecurity-magazine.com>.

[15] Ibid.

[16] Ibid.

[17] Camden.

Risks in Energy – Oil and Gas Industry

Abbas Khambati

August 2012

Abstract: *The oil and gas industry is often rife with uncertainties and risks – therefore, Abbas presents an overview of the risk environment to help identify and quantify the risks from a public and private sector perspective. The paper examines the risks faced by the oil and gas industry and then provides suggestions for mitigation.*

Introduction

With advancements in technology, it often feels as if the world is becoming a smaller place. The growing economy brings a plethora of opportunities, but it also brings greater interdependence among different sectors and hence greater risks. How businesses respond to the new threats is critical in determining the existence of a better tomorrow. The world is increasingly volatile - the environment is prone to unexpected and unprecedented events, which may be in the form of natural disasters, terrorist attacks, governmental change, and public health crises. All these can cause economic and political instability across the globe. A fire at a metal manufacturing plant in New Orleans can force a leading European manufacturer out of the cell phone business, and similarly social unrest in Africa can push up the global price of crude oil. This interconnectedness in the world economy is increasingly an accepted part of conventional wisdom, but what is less obvious is the "misalignment" created by the differential experiences and impacts of risks, and the resulting disconnect between those affected by a risk and those who can mitigate a risk.[1]

One of the biggest risks that economies face today is depletion of natural resources due to inappropriate or excessive usage. These resources are primarily used for fuelling the economy in a variety of ways. Cooking food, heating a house, street lighting, running a hospital, operating a factory – all these require energy. Energy is at the heart of everybody's part of life and a decisive factor for economic competitiveness and growth. Nations have established a wide spread of industries that are involved in harnessing energy resources and formalized the operational risk-measurement procedures that are incorporated in day-to-day activities. Additionally, governments have carved out niche "energy" sectors for these industries, often governed by a special set of policies and regulations. The U.S. energy infrastructure fuels the nation's economy in the 21st century. Without a stable energy supply, health and welfare is threatened and the U.S. economy cannot function.[2] More than 80 percent of the country's energy infrastructure is owned by the private sector.[3] Clearly, the U.S. government largely relies on the private sector for meeting its energy demands and there is a growing dependency as well. The energy infrastructure is divided into three interrelated segments: electricity, petroleum, and natural gas.[4] This paper will discuss the risks associated within the petroleum and natural gas sectors from both a governmental as well as a private sector perspective.

Role of the Government

Petroleum and natural gas comprise one of the most critical focus-areas of the government in the energy sector, with the nation importing about 45 percent of total domestic oil demand.[5] This implies trading more than $1 billion offshore daily.[6] The federal body in charge of overseeing the oil and gas regulations in the U.S. is the Department of Energy (DOE). The DOE is also responsible for overseeing infrastructure operations; encouraging public and private investments; and planning, recommending, and overseeing policies for the oil and gas industry. The government plays an important role in developing technologies through research and development, and the private sector has traditionally driven setting up infrastructure as well as building ties with other global economies to facilitate information sharing, scaling to commercial deployment and operations. Furthermore, the government alone cannot finance large-scale energy transformation; total annual investment in the U.S. energy system totaled $200 billion, whereas the DOE's entire annual budget, including basic research, energy research, waste cleanup, and nuclear security, topped out at $25 billion, which is no more than the capital budget for a single large energy company.[7] Thus, the private sector collaborates with the government to run the energy sector and ensure profitability in the process.

Government Risks in the Oil and Gas Sector

The DOE is the main regulatory body that governs policies for oil and gas in the U.S. It is important for the DOE to cushion the impact that global events in the energy market have on the U.S. market, and support stability in the oil and gas industries. In order to accomplish this, the agency constantly monitors and mitigates risks associated with this volatile industry.

The major risks include:

Environment, Health and Safety Risk – The impact of the 2010 British Petroleum (BP) deep-sea oil rig explosion at the Macondo site in the Gulf of Mexico continues to be felt by the U.S. oil and gas industry. The accident not only involved loss of lives, but also devastated the ecosystem in the area, the surrounding waters, and beyond. The fallout damaged local industries and economies, and proved to have long-term consequences. The government regulatory agencies were blamed for allowing the set up and operations of dangerous drilling sites like these all over the Gulf and the East Coast. Oil spill incidents such as the BP spill have had a global effect with many other countries increasing scrutiny and reviewing policies related to offshore drilling, spurred by the accidents that have proven to be hazardous to the environment and local economies. The tightening safety and environmental guidelines are requiring massive investment by operators in the oil and gas industry, an unwelcome trend.

Price Volatility – Political and social unrest in oil-rich Middle East and North Africa countries often results in volatile oil prices. Additional demand shocks can be triggered by a range of global economic crises. Since the U.S. imports a major part of its oil and gas reserves, a change in the foreign exchange currency market could also mean fluctuations in the price range of billions of dollars.

Inability to Find Alternatives in Case of Failure - The U.S. Department of Energy (DOE) is constantly faced with the challenge of reducing dependency on non-sustainable sources of energy. The challenge is to move from non-renewable sources such as oil and gas towards sustainable renewable sources of energy. Due to the finite nature of oil and gas extraction, as wells dry up the oil and gas industry continues to push for expanding deep sea drilling operations, presenting higher risks.

Natural Disasters and Extreme Weather Conditions - The DOE is also faced with concerns about private companies drilling offshore in deep waters where tropical storms and hurricanes can have serious consequences on production as well as on the environment.

These are some of the major risks that the DOE faces constantly. However, other risks like economic stability concerns, changes in demand for oil and gas, and the impact of climatic change are also part of the risk portfolio that the DOE manages.

Role of the Private Sector

The private sector is pivotal in collaborating with the government with capital, infrastructure, and technology to set up industries that harness the resources that would fuel the economy of the nation. Major companies in the U.S. that are major players in the private sector are Exxon-Mobil, Chevron, and BP. The role of the private sector is driven by regulations and policies, since companies are governed by the

DOE. Although the private sector is profit driven, it is necessary to combine the interests of the private sector with the priorities of the public sector to create an effective energy sector.

Private Sector Risks in the Oil and Gas Sector

The risks identified in the private sector largely depend on the policies and regulations of the government. In addition, environmental factors contribute to a majority of the risks.

Some of the identified risks are:

Operational Complexity - Private sector oil and gas companies are operating in increasingly remote geographical locations and harsher environmental conditions for offshore drilling operations. Tighter safety and environmental guidelines are requiring massive capital investments from the industry.

Environmental Restrictions and Regulations – Legislation concerning greenhouse gas emissions and climate changes, along with concern about the long-term impact of hydraulic drilling in oceans, serves as a source of constant risk to the oil and gas industry.

Inadequate Liquidity or Access to Capital – A capital-intensive industry, oil and gas companies must not only be concerned about their individual financial resources. Threats to the financial health of industry partners, customers, vendors, and suppliers together contribute to the industry's risks.

General Industry Competition and Constantly Changing Market Scenario - With government agencies imposing new regulations, profit margins may be pressured, leading to increased competitiveness amongst oil companies. Industry participants seek to capture, retain, and grow market share.

Shortage of Experts - The oil and gas industry is also facing a shortage of technical expertise. The looming shortage of talent spans multiple departments in this industry - notably Operations (81 percent), Information Technology (61 percent), Risk and Regulatory (62 percent) and Research and Development (60 percent).[8] These areas are mainly involved in analyzing the scientific and engineering data used in exploration and production of oil and gas.

Government Regulation and Sector-Specific Controls

In January 2009, the U.S. Department of Homeland Security (DHS) announced a revised version of the National Infrastructure Protection Plan (NIPP), a comprehensive risk management framework that defines critical infrastructure protection (CIP) roles and responsibilities for all levels of government, private industry, and other sector partners.[9] The NIPP builds on the principles of the President's National Strategy for Homeland Security and strategies for the protection of critical infrastructure and key resources (CIKR).

The U.S. Department of Energy (DOE) has been designated as the Sector-Specific Agency (SSA) for the energy sector and has developed the Sector Specific Plan (SSP) for the energy sector. The energy SSP is based mainly on the risk management framework defined in the NIPP.

The major constituents of the NIPP management framework involved the process of:

Setting Goals and Objectives → *Identifying Assets Systems and Networks* → *Assess Risks* → *Prioritize* → *Implement Programs* → *Measuring Effectiveness.* [10]

The U.S. government also plays a major role in regulating policies based on environmental concerns for the oil and gas industry. Oil and gas resources are not a sustainable source of energy – only a finite amount of oil and gas can be extracted before the source runs "dry." Therefore, there is a constant effort by oil and gas companies to authorize drilling in deeper seas and explore potential sites. Many new regulations from the government try to control the operations of these companies. For example, a recent policy addition by the Obama administration tightened regulations on the oil and gas industry by requiring drillers to capture emissions of certain air pollutants released from new wells.[11] The rule will require all oil and gas companies to capture the volatile organic compounds that are emitted during the final stages of well construction, including during the process of hydraulic fracturing.[12] Similar measures like these have been implemented by the government to ensure a cleaner, greener and safer environment for the oil and gas industry.

Dependency Amongst Sectors

The oil and gas industry accounts for the majority of the world's energy generation. While critics challenge the use and dependency on fossil fuels, without them lights would go out and vehicles would stop running. Virtually all the critical sectors ranging from food and agriculture to banking and finance depend heavily on the energy sector, and currently oil and gas production drives the industry. In short, the economic growth of the nation is largely dependent on the oil and gas industry.

Risk Mitigation for the Government Sector

In order to balance the many dependencies on the oil and gas industry, the U.S. government must continue to engage with the private sector. This requires the government to take the private sector mindset into consideration, and expect a more business-driven environment. It is also important to ensure that environment and public heath safety standards are maintained at the same time.

Increased Audits for Health and Environment Safety Risks - It is pertinent for the Department of Energy to conduct regular mandatory audits and make maintenance a requirement. It is also important to periodically review control systems and address defects that surface. Control systems that are put into place for disaster and crisis situations should be audited. These systems can be in the form of software systems, pre-setup hardware equipment or even calibrated alarm systems that respond to critical alerts

Predictable Policies - The first and most important consideration is predictability. Given the extended timelines standard in the oil and gas industry, policies that are unclear or alter every few years will hinder industry growth. Further, it is important that the policies are well considered and streamlined towards the goals of the economy on a whole. Industry participants do not want to be pursuing policies and procedures that are not optimal in terms of technology, economics, or environmental impact.

Test New Technologies - The DOE's advanced National Laboratories could play a major role in shaping the use of new technologies in the industry and thus mitigate risks related to technology. This could be achieved by testing new technologies at the DOE's scientific facilities itself. The results could provide significant insight into operations and mechanisms at scale. For example, a micro-grid test bed where various demand-side technologies can be tested in real environments, or combustion facilities where technologies for gas treatment, CO_2 absorption, and other components could be tested at commercial scale and operational conditions would reduce uncertainties and risks surrounding the deployment of new technologies.[13]

Loan Guarantees for Capital Risk - To address capital risk, the DOE has been executing loan guarantees. This would help extend financial stability in an ever changing and competitive market. It would also serve as an incentive for the industry to invest in the latest technology to reduce the chances of errors and blunders.

Use of Simulation – Government research departments can use simulation to mitigate risk.

Simulation is currently used in the federal science and weapons programs for testing nuclear arms for defense purposes. The U.S. is at the forefront of applying high-performance computing to realistic physical models. Therefore, the government should focus on developing simulation capabilities in the energy sector. Simulating the mechanics of devices that would be instrumental in oil and gas industry production would help optimize the designs, operation, and technology transitions.

Green Business Continuity Plan - The DOE should ensure that its regulations involve a mandatory business continuity plan that includes a plan for how industry operators will respond to crisis, while minimizing possible damages to the environment and its ecosystem. The continuity plan is also necessary to protect the production cycles of oil and gas extraction, cushioning the industry against the immediate effects of a crisis.

Risk Mitigation for the Private Sector

Constantly changing and complicated governmental policies pressure private sector companies to look for superior ways to manage and monitor risk and controls for reducing deviations, human-error, and redundant activities.

Preventing Non-Compliance - Non-compliance is a risk that oil and gas companies cannot avoid with the regulatory environment increasing. Timely reporting on operations and accidents is required, as well as risk mitigation plans for critical operations like drilling must be prepared and reviewed well in advance. Companies need to ensure that important documents, including the approvals for drilling, building and maintaining the oil and gas wells, are made available throughout the company and across enterprise boundaries to curtail risk and ensure compliance.

Real-Time Monitoring and Predictive Maintenance - Oil and gas firms generally follow a defensive approach and often suffer major losses due to a failure to identify risks in a timely manner. Undiscovered exposures can result in massive damages in terms of money as well as reputation. By guarding against situations where collective risk exposure exceeds risk appetite, a company can help prevent such situations. Controls should be put into place to help mitigate risks in real time using alerts.

Collaborative Planning, Operations, and Decision-Making - It is important for process owners to take direct responsibility for intensive planning and managing controls. To eliminate risks from deviations in procedures, miscalculations and redundant activities, compliance and controls should be made consistent across an enterprise using a centralized framework and collaborative environment. It is also helpful to reduce non-productive time and enhance production along with reduction of both economic and environmental health and safety risks. To facilitate this, companies should create a stronger and more comprehensive connection between field operations staff and remote experts. IT is one of the most important assets an energy company can have for mitigating risks. Automation of secure manual control systems in a company can be done with the help of a robust IT system.

Conclusion

The oil and gas industry has numerous complexities; there are distinctions and aspects that may not be readily apparent to most people not directly involved with the energy industry. It requires a long-term vision as well as continuous partnership between the government and private sectors to set up a safe and sustainable atmosphere for a prosperous and energy efficient industry. Secondly, the government's key role in creating change in the energy system is partly to mitigate risk for the private sector. Setting a predictable and well-constructed foundation of policies and economics is the most important thing the government can do.[14] Beyond that, the DOE should facilitate large-scale demonstration projects, support research, and the transfer of new technologies into industry.

---

[1] Wyman, Oliver. "Realigning Risks and Rewards in the Energy Sector." Oliver Wyman. Jan.
2006. Accessed 4 Jun. 2012 <www.mmc.com>

[2] "18 Critical Infrastructure Sectors and Key Resources." Alabama Fusion Center, State of Alabama. n.d. Accessed 4
Jun. 2012 <www.fusion.alabama.gov>

[3] *Energy Sector: Critical Infrastructure.* U.S. Department of Homeland Security. n.d. Accessed 02 Aug. 2012 <www.dhs.gov>.

[4] "Critical Infrastructure Protection Topics." The National Institute for Hometown Security. n.d. Accessed 4 Jun. 2012 <www.thenihs.org>.

[5] Longley, Robert. "Should Obama Take Credit for U.S. Oil Production Hike?" *About.Com.* n.d. Accessed 02 Aug. 2012 <usgovinfo.about.com>

[6] Ibid.

[7] Gopstein, Avi M. and Steven E. Koonin. "Accelerating the Pace of Energy Change." *Issues in Science and Technology - Winter 2011.* Jan. 2011. Accessed 4 Jun. 2012 <www.issues.org>.

[8] "Deloitte: Oil and Gas Sector Faces Talent Shortage." Mediaquest FZ LLC. 10 May 2012. Accessed 4 Jun., 2012 <www.ameinfo.com>.

[9] "Energy Sector-Specific Plan: An Annex to the National Infrastructure Protection Plan, 2010." *Homeland Security Digital Library.* n.d. Accessed 4 Jun. 2012 < www.hsdl.org>.

[10] "Sector-Specific Plans." U.S. Department of Homeland Security. n.d. Accessed 02 Aug. 2012 <www.dhs.gov>.

[11] Hargreaves, Steve. "Obama Tightens Oil and Gas Drilling Regulations." *Cable News Network.* 18 Apr. 2012. Accessed 02 Aug. 2012 <money.cnn.com>.

[12] Ibid.

[13] Gopstein.

[14] Ibid.

Critical Infrastructure Protection Healthcare and Public Health

Divya Yadav

May 2013

Abstract: *With the Patient Protection and Affordable Care Act in the forefront of many public discussions, healthcare is a hot topic in 2013. Divya takes a behind-the-scenes look at the underlying infrastructure supporting the healthcare industry and public healthcare sector. After identifying risks in both the private and public sectors, and the interdependencies that cross multiple sectors, Divya recommends possible steps for increasing resiliency of U.S. healthcare infrastructure.*

Introduction

Critical infrastructure are the "assets, systems, and networks, whether physical or virtual, so vital to the U.S. that their incapacitation or destruction would have a debilitating effect on security, national economic security, public health or safety, or any combination thereof."[1] The U.S. identifies 16 such critical infrastructures that are important to the existence and wellbeing of its citizens. Critical infrastructure protections include the measures that are in place to protect these critical infrastructure systems. Healthcare is one of the 16[*] identified critical infrastructures, and a failure in the proper functioning of healthcare systems can result in disaster. Healthcare in U.S. continues to be a topic of debate, particularly due to recent policies put in place by the government. This paper reflects on the risks associated with public and private healthcare in order to provide shareholder and customer value. Emerging and prevalent risks within healthcare can potentially damage the system, and the U.S. government cannot afford to take such risks. Risks in healthcare include operational, financial, environmental, clinical, and reputational risks. In order to identify potential risks and build a robust operational risk framework, it is important to clearly specify the objectives and vision.

Risks in the U.S. Public Healthcare System

The government delivers healthcare services in the U.S. to specific demographics via the Medicare, Medicaid, and Veterans' programs. These programs provide services beyond healthcare for the elderly, the poor, children, veterans, public sector employees, and the disabled. The current structure of public

---

[*] The *Presidential Policy Directive 21 (PPD-21): Critical Infrastructure Security and Resilience* changed the number of critical infrastructure sectors to 16 in February 2013 (from the 18 as defined by the Homeland Security Presidential Directive 7 of December 2003, referenced in earlier research notes in this collection).

healthcare in the country is such it faces several operational risks for its existence.

Limited Resources: Shortage of clinicians and physicians is one of the risks associated with existing public healthcare programs. Some attribute the cause to high administrative costs and low reimbursement rates for providers. Government efforts at cost reductions often targeted towards Medicare and Medicaid, citing limited resources. Cuts in funding and resources pose severe risk to healthcare systems, particularly if high volumes of patients visit the emergency rooms of hospitals and medical centers. Additionally, lingering economic uncertainty continues to put strain on students pursuing medical degrees. As the level of pay associated with public healthcare programs goes down and the cost of education rises, a growing number of medical students report that the high level of effort required to attain a medical license may not be worth the resources and effort.[2] If the number of medical professionals willing to serve patients through the public healthcare programs continues to decline, the strain on the system will continue to increase.

Limited Services and Coverage of Health Plan: Healthcare services viewed as discretionary - such as cosmetic surgery - are as a rule not covered by public healthcare programs. The limited nature of coverage creates potential risk for patients, who may genuinely require services not covered by the programs. For example, a patient may require facial reconstruction-related surgeries if involved in a serious accident. These limitations put the life of people at risk that might need such procedures, and there should be some guidelines and exceptions in place pertaining to these procedures in order to help people attain the best care and treatment as possible.[3]

Information System Infrastructure and Electronic Health Records Implementation: Public healthcare suffers in terms of access and use of consistent and reliable technology and information system, primarily due to the lack of up-front investment funds available.

Information Security and Data Privacy Concerns: There have been numerous instances of security breaches in public healthcare systems, compromising patient information. The incidents primarily stem from the inability to protect the networks from external attacks. Many systems lack sufficient controls for network access, privileges and roles, heightening the risks to healthcare systems.

Internal and External Fraud: Fraudulent activities related to Medicare/Medicaid fraud pose a threat to public healthcare. Instances of Medicare fraud have led to an increase in the total Medicare spending from the federal government. Phantom billing, patient billing and upcoding scheme, and bundling are some of the potential risks and fraud that are part of internal fraud in public healthcare system. In order to address these risks, the government has implemented the use of data analytics and increased scrutiny of billing patterns.

Risks in the U.S. Private Healthcare System

The private sector remains the primary provider of healthcare services in U.S., with the majority of healthcare insurance coverage provided by employee-sponsored plans. Individuals may also purchase healthcare insurance, or pay for healthcare services directly if they have no healthcare insurance.

Decentralized Patient Healthcare Information: There is no central repository of healthcare data for private healthcare providers. This places the burden of retaining and organizing healthcare data on individual patients, across various providers and healthcare centers. Each healthcare provider may track a patient, creating multiple healthcare records for one individual across many different systems. This decentralized method leads to increase in overhead administrative costs and often results in substantial errors and gaps in patient healthcare information. One way to reduce these risks to patient healthcare data would be for healthcare providers to collaborate and create a centralized repository for storing and accessing patient healthcare information.[4]

No Unification in Billing and Coding Process: Billing processes for private healthcare can be very complex and extensive. The back-and-forth interactions between healthcare providers, patients and insurance companies can make healthcare billing and insurance claims processing very lengthy. Healthcare providers have different methods and coding processes for billing their services and submitting claims to insurance companies. The varying processes often leave patients frustrated, confused and uninformed about the information provided on billing invoices.

High Costs of Services: The cost of healthcare services in a private system can become very high, particularly since hospitals and healthcare centers can control pricing of provided services. While healthcare insurance can mitigate the costs, risks include high prices and premiums that many citizens face after catastrophic illness that put them on the verge of bankruptcy.[5]

Emerging Risks due to Social Media and Cloud Computing: Studies have found that hospitals in general are not equipped for handling social media issues. Social media can make or break a brand and healthcare should be careful how they deal with it and the risks associated with it in terms of their brand building. Cloud computing is another area of concern for the healthcare. Not having sophisticated systems in place further propagates the problems. Cloud security is a very relevant issue and healthcare providers should consult risk consultants to ensure proper controls in place for mapping controls to their specific cloud providers, which ensures data integrity and smooth functioning.

Effectiveness of Government Regulations in the Healthcare Sector

Regulations in healthcare are provided by the U.S. Department of Health and Human Services (DHH), which fosters many of the agencies that regulate healthcare within U.S. There are some basic regulations that the healthcare industry is expected to comply with and the effectiveness of these regulations is something reflected upon in this paper.

Regulation of Healthcare Professionals: Medical licenses are permitted at the state level and these laws are governed by the American Medical Association. The key point to note in this regulation is that while it does enhance the quality of practitioners by reducing the number of applications, it allows a limited number of practitioners to raise costs. Another potential flaw with this regulation is that if a practitioner is denied a license in one state, they have the complete freedom to go and attain a license in a different state. This information is controlled centrally through National Practitioner Data Bank, but studies suggest it is not well coordinated and loss of information provides a loophole in the system.[6]

Regulation of Healthcare Institutions Such as Hospitals and Other Medical Facilities: Regulations are in place for measuring the quality of patient care in hospitals. However, challenges arise in deciding on a basic framework to measure and define clear metrics for measuring the quality of care. The problem is there are no specific metrics and the frameworks for measuring healthcare quality are still not mature enough to continue making successful predictions. "Regulation of institutional quality presents an opportunity to consider the challenges in the definition and measurement of this attribute."[7] The other significant aspect of quality control is to provide services to the uninsured and not turn them away in times of emergency due to lack of funds. Some patients - knowing that they will not be denied a treatment - visit these emergency cares for minor treatments, delaying the reimbursements for hospital and putting them under financial pressure. Consequently, it is very important to devise regulation that keeps a proper check on quality, access, and cost.

Regulation on Healthcare Finance Administration: American healthcare is particularly complex in terms of its financial administration. Private and public healthcare is intertwined and controlled at a federal level that adds further to the complexity. Employer based insurance puts people without employment at a severe disadvantage and also puts a financial burden on the firms to offer insurance and have an entire structure build around it, especially tough for startups and not for profits to implement such a structure. A universal healthcare taken care of by government would serve as a good alternative to streamline financial operations but different organizations and individuals have different views about it.[8]

Regulation of Drugs and Healthcare Products: Drugs and healthcare products need to be evaluated by regulators before they hit the market. FDA ensures proper guidelines but according to manufacturers, the FDA process is a long, rigorous, and expensive method for completing assessments. An effective regulation needs to be in place to balance out the costs that speeds up the production and marketing of the drugs without comprising the quality of the drugs.[9]

Regulations in IT: IT has changed the way healthcare is provided and the way patients; clinicians and physicians communicate with each other. Programs such as HIPAA are put in place to effectively monitor that patient information is not being compromised. IT regulatory is still undergoing many formulations and the areas of inclusions are: role of data analytics and how comfortable patients are in making the information available public.[10]

Dependencies

Several sectors depend on healthcare (as healthcare depends on many sectors), and disruptions in operations can have serious consequences. Emergency Services Sector is highly dependent on healthcare sector. "Preparedness of hospitals and other medical facilities comes into picture in the wake of natural disasters, disease outbreaks, casualties from terrorist attacks and so on. Preparing hospitals, healthcare systems and their partners to prevent, respond to, and rapidly recover from these threats is critical for protecting and securing our Nation's healthcare system and public health infrastructure."[11] Operability of healthcare depends notably on the functional capability of other basic infrastructural services like electricity, water supply, information and telecommunication technologies, transport and logistics, and specialized staff. These interdependencies are a key element for the security of healthcare facilities in crises.[12]

Government should put in place policies that try to secure hospitals and health centers dependency on other critical infrastructure. "In many cases the hospitals simply rely on the safety measures of the public utility company which is a potential flaw and can severely affect the business continuity in wake of disasters. Similar conclusions can be drawn from the dependency on specialized staff. The situation in the transport/logistics sector is very hospital specific because every facility has its individual organizational solutions that depend on the spatial conditions, dimensions of the facility, and other similar factors."[13]

There are certain internal dependencies that exist within the hospitals such as dependencies between important processes and services in hospitals and basic infrastructure. Diagnostics, medical equipment and their proper cleaning, treatment, pharmacy, laboratory results are some of the practices that a healthcare center depends upon for its day to day functioning and pose a vulnerable situation for health centers. It is important to understand all external and internal interdependencies between sectors and systems and devise business continuity, roles, and responsibilities and a risk communications plan for all the sectors so they are equipped to work together when the need arises.

Steps Towards Resiliency

"Resilience is the intrinsic ability of a system to adjust its functioning prior to, during, or following changes and disturbances so that it can sustain required operations, even after a major mishap or in the presence of continuous stress."[14]

Risks exist with every critical infrastructure and healthcare system is no exception. The important point is to analyze all those risks, have a disaster cycle in place that mitigates those risks, and have a recovery plan to ensure resiliency of the healthcare system. To ensure backup, recovery and smooth transition from a failure a proper risk management framework needs to be in place that addresses these failures and steps to quickly recover from such catastrophic disasters.

Integration of IT and healthcare has led to increase in risks associated with this sector. Patient records and information stored in cloud pose a risk of possible misadventures such as loss of information and misrepresentation of information that can have severe consequences for providing patient care. Therefore, it is very important to have a system level approach in place that gives proper regard to safety of information systems.

Many regard healthcare system in the U.S. to be a fragmented system, as there is no unification of data and patient information amongst private healthcare providers. "An estimated 60 million patients in the U.S. suffer from two or more chronic conditions and are particularly affected by this disconnection among clinical care specialties. Connectivity, integrated care, and coordination are inadequate nationwide at all stages of illness treatment."[15] These gaps need to be identified and a system needs to be in place that captures all patient information and data from private healthcare providers. Hospitals can leverage the use of cloud computing and store information; have enough backups to ensure consistent information. Policies, procedures, and internal controls need to be in place to ensure cloud safety. Information Security policy, Incident Management plan, Vulnerability scans and penetration testing, real time access to cloud providers management platform and dashboards are some of the controls that can be put in place to ensure proper functioning of cloud computing services.

"Complex equipment and information systems can also contribute to brittleness or resilience."[16] These systems are often installed in Intensive Care Units that offer acute patient care and recent reports of failures indicate that practitioners were faced with unexpected results from automation of IT and these failures demonstrate a poor understanding of the work settings they are intended to support. "Opaque systems that offer poor feedback and low transparency undermine resilience and increase brittleness. There is a need to create new visualizations that provide improved feedback and observation to help people recognize when events challenge current plans in progress."[17]

Recent economic meltdown and financial pressures have put a barrier on Emergency Department Response to respond effectively. "The system has to stretch in response to increasing demands to avoid an accumulation of gaps that would lead to a system failure."[18] Emergency Departments have to be able to stretch their strategies on the fly when faced with emergencies and utilize the capability of their resources to meet the needs of the patients.

A second step to ensure resiliency in healthcare would be to bring the stakeholders of all critical Infrastructure systems together, foster an effective critical infrastructure protection program that addresses dependencies amongst the systems, and provide measures that can be beneficial for the citizens in the wake of an emergency. Social media and social networking are hot topics for businesses these days, and the pace of information sharing has been changed forever. Now with technologies and services ranging from Facebook, Twitter, LinkedIn, blogs, texting, instant messaging, Flickr – the list is ongoing and ever growing. These new modes of communication are now allowing people to share Immediate and unfiltered content. Moreover, this has raised many questions, debates, and problems for companies and organizations that are struggling to keep up with the pace and shifts that drive the dynamic world of electronic communications.

[1] "Critical Infrastructure." Department of Homeland Security. n. d. Accessed 10 Mar. 2013 <www.dhs.gov>.

[2] *Assessment of Key Risks for Hospitals and Healthcare Systems – Spring 2010.* KPMG, Healthcare & Pharmaceutical Institute, KPMG LLP. Jul. 2010. Accessed 10 Mar. 2013 <www.kpmg.com>.

[3] Assessment.

[4] Health Care Internal Audit: Identifying Prevalent Risks within Your Organization. McGladrey. 2011. Accessed 10 Mar. 2013 <www.mcgladrey.com>.

[5] *Public vs. Private Health Care.* Ehow.com. n.d. Accessed 10 Mar. 2013 <www.ehow.com>

[6] Field, Robert. I. Teacher's Guide for Healthcare Regulation in America: Complexity, Confrontation and Compromise. Aug. 2007. p. 5. Accessed 13 Mar. 2013 <www.healthcareregulation.net>.

[7] Field, p. 7.

[8] Field, p. 11.

[9] Field, p. 14.

[10] Field, p. 22.

[11] *Healthcare Preparedness Capabilities.* Public Health Emergency, U.S. Department of Health & Human Services. 10 Jan. 2012. Accessed 10 Mar. 2013 <www.phe.gov>.

[12] Riegel, Christopher. Risk Assessment and Critical Infrastructure Protection in Health Care Facilities: Reducing

Social Vulnerability. Institute for Environment and Human Security, United
Nations University. Aug. 2007. Accessed 10 Mar. 2013
<www.ehs.unu.edu>.

[13] Riegel.

[14] Nemeth, Christopher, Robert Wears, David Woods, Erik Hollnagle, Richard
Cook. *Minding the Gaps: Creating Resilience in Health Care.*
Advances in Patient Safety, Agency for Healthcare Research and
Quality. Aug. 2008. Accessed 10 Mar. 2013 <www.ahrq.gov>.

[15] Riegel.

[16] Nemeth.

[17] Nemeth.

[18] Nemeth.

Chapter II
Privacy

Understanding Google's Privacy Policy Change

Andrew H. R. Hansen
March 2012

Abstract: *Andrew examines the transition Google made in 2012 to merge all the different privacy policies from over sixty products and services into one comprehensive policy. This change allowed Google to compile and provide detailed profiles of its users. Many in the online community accused Google of privacy violation; Google disagreed, saying user privacy is still protected under the merger while service is improved. For those uncomfortable with the changes, Andrew provides recommendations for ways to minimize online profile.*

Introduction

"If you're not paying for something, you're not the customer; you're the product being sold."[1] This statement definitely captures the essence of user interactions with organizations like Google and Facebook. Over the past several years, Internet users have steadily become more aware of how their online activity is monitored, gathered, analyzed, and used to provide targeted advertisements and a personalized web experience. On March 1, 2012, Google made the most dramatic changes yet to its privacy policy, a move that has caused anger and anxiety among Internet activists, and added fuel to the debate concerning user privacy. This research note will discuss the changes to Google's privacy policy, outline some of the possible implications, discuss government responses and suggest ways users can minimize their online profile.

How Google Makes Money

To begin with, it is important to understand how Google makes money, and why the tech firm is interested in acquiring user information. The vast majority of Google revenue is generated through selling advertisements. Google has developed several different models and methods for selling advertisements and has seen enormous success through its efforts. The advertising methods will not be discussed in this research note, but the important element to understand is that the more information Google knows about its users, the ability to target ads specifically engineered to their interests increases, and so does the value of those ads.

From its founding in 1998, Google has evolved into a huge corporation, offering several different products and services. Just to name a few: Google search, Gmail, YouTube, Google Earth, Google+, Blogger, Google Maps, Picasa, Google Docs, and now Android (Google's mobile phone operating system). For most users, it would take deliberate effort to use the Internet and avoid these products and services.[2]

Changes to Google's Privacy Policy

Under Google's former policy, user information gathered by one Google entity was kept separate from information gathered by another. For example, information collected from Google search, was kept separate from information collected from Gmail or YouTube. In addition, each of these different services had separate privacy policies.[3] Under the new policy, however, "over 60 products across the Google portfolio will scrap their separate privacy policies and combine into one."[4]

It is important to note that the new policy does not allow Google to collect more information about its users, but it does allow Google to do more with the information they have already been gathering.[5] Consolidating and analyzing the user information in this way allows Google to "laser-target ads at its users."[6]

Alan Simpson, vice president of policy for Common Sense Media, an advocacy group for Internet safety issues says that these privacy changes "are taking place in the midst of a data arms race between Facebook, Google and other companies in the space… They're all working to gather as much data and personal information as they can and figuring out ways that they will use our data to develop a better advertising market."[7]

Online Response

These changes have raised several concerning issues for privacy advocates. To begin with, there is no way for users to opt out of these changes, a move which many feel will result in users being forced to "share data about themselves that they may not want shared, given a proper choice."[8] In addition to not offering an opt out feature, if users do not want their Gmail and Google searches combining to create a detailed personal profile, the only remedy Google is currently offering is to stop using its services.[9] Many companies and individuals have come to rely on these Google services, and the fact that all users are required to submit to these new terms or stop using Google services, is not sitting well with many users. In a non-scientific online poll conducted by the Washington Post, of the 13,541 readers who took the survey, "66 percent said they would cancel their Google accounts because of the changes."[10]

Another major concern receiving attention is the effect of the policy change on those who have Android-powered mobile phones. A user may have a choice when it comes to what search engine or email service provider they choose, but to those customers who already own an Android smartphone, the option of accepting the policy or not using Google's services means they would have to give up their phone. One prominent privacy campaigner claimed that "the changes are a significant infringement of my right to privacy and I do not consent to Google being able to use my data in such a way."[11] Consequently, this user filed a lawsuit against Google for the cost of his Android powered phone, arguing that the new policy represents an unfair change in contract terms and will force him to buy a new smartphone.[12]

Government Response

The policy change has garnered similar criticism from members of governments in both the U.S. and Europe. On February 22, attorneys general from 36 different states issued a letter to Google reprimanding them for what they say is unfair behavior. The letter had some strong words regarding Google's approach:

"Google's new privacy policy goes against a respect for privacy that Google has carefully cultivated as a way to attract consumers. It rings hollow to call (the ability of users) to exit the Google products ecosystem a 'choice' in an Internet economy where the clear majority of all Internet users use – and frequently rely on – at least one Google product on a regular basis."[13]

In addition, the letter brought to attention the Android smartphone concern, saying many "will find it 'virtually impossible' to escape the policy without ditching their phones."[14]

International governments have also vocalized their concerns about the policy change. In early February, shortly after Google issued the policy change announcement, European governments, with support from the top justice official in the Europeans Union (E.U.), asked Google to halt the coming policy changes, while they "investigate the implications for personal data."[15] In a letter to Google chief executive Larry Page, E.U. authorities called for "a pause in the interest of ensuring that there can be no misunderstanding about Google's commitments to information rights of their users and E.U. citizens."[16]

Along with this E.U. pressure, Commission Nationale de l'Informatique et des Libertes (CNIL), a French data protection watchdog, also issued a letter to Google, "casting doubt on the legality of the private policy, and informing Google that it would lead a Europe-wide investigation."[17] European Union Justice Commissioner Viviane Reding stated, "All companies that offer services to European consumers must provide their customers with clear information about their policy. In Europe, consumers must be able to make informed decisions about using Internet-based services."[18] He went on to add, "It is unfortunate that Google has gone ahead with the new policy before addressing the French data protection authority's concern."[19]

Google's Position

According to Google's user privacy director Alma Whitten, Google just wants to "use the information you already trust us with to make your experience better."[20] By combining information across all of Google's services, they feel they will be able to provide a richer customer experience. Whitten went on to say, "If you don't think information sharing will improve your experience, you don't need to sign in to use services like Search, Maps and YouTube."[21] Whitten also pointed out that even if you are signed in to a Google account you can "edit or turn off your search history, control the way Google tailors ads to your interests and browse the Web 'incognito'* using Chrome."[22]

In response to the concerns raised by the European Union Google has said it was happy to answer questions from Europe's data protection authorities. In late February, Google responded via a blog post

---

* According to a Google Chrome tutorial, browsing "incognito" means that "webpages that you open and files downloaded while you are incognito won't be logged in your browsing and download histories; all new cookies are deleted after you close the incognito window."

saying, "while our privacy policies will change on 1st March, our commitment to our privacy principles is as strong as ever... We are confident that our new simple, clear and transparent privacy policy respects all European data protection laws and principles."[23]

Minimizing Your Online Profile

Alma Whitten's comments regarding not signing in to Google accounts suggest that there are ways to minimize the information Google is able to capture. The following list of suggestions and commentary is taken from an article[24] written by CNN's Doug Gross, and provides recommendations for how users can help take control the information Google is able to capture.

- *Do not sign in.* Many of Google's services – most notably search, YouTube and Maps – do not require you to sign in to use them. If you are not logged in, via Gmail or Google+, for example, Google does not know who you are and cannot add data to your profile.
- *Clear your Google search history.* Deleting your history will not prevent Google from using the information internally. Nevertheless, it will limit the amount of time that it is fully accessible. After 18 months, the data becomes anonymous again and will not be used as part of your profile.

- *Clear your YouTube history.*
- *Clear your browsing history on Google Chrome*
- *Erase your Google Chat Log.* When you start a chat with someone, you can make the conversation "off the record." Off-the-record chats will not be stored in your chat history or the history of the person with whom you are talking. All chats with that person will remain off the record until you change the status.

Conclusion

For years Google has operated under the informal motto of "Don't be evil." Whether you feel that these recent changes in privacy policy are a violation of that motto, or if you appreciate the fact that with these changes Google will now likely offer better service, the important thing to understand is how companies like Google and Facebook are using your data, and make informed consumer decisions. The reality is that we simply do not know all the ways the information gathered on us could potentially affect our lives. In the meantime, erring on the side of caution and minimizing your online profile, may just prove to be worth the extra effort.

---

[1] Gibbs, Mark. "You are the Product for The Google." *ComputerWorld.* 2 Mar. 2012. Accessed 8 Mar. 2012 <www.computerworld.com>.

[2] Gaudin, Sharon. "Google Stirs up Privacy Hornet's Nest." *ComputerWorld.* 26 Jan. 2012. Accessed 8 Mar. 2012 <www.computerworld.com>.

[3] Ngak, Chenda. "Google's Privacy Policy Change Takes Effect." *CBS News.* 1 Mar. 2012. Accessed 8 Mar.

2012 <www.cbsnews.com>.

[4] Ibid.

[5] Gaudin.

[6] Ibid.

[7] Bosker, Bianca. "Google Privacy Policy Changing for Everyone: So What's Really Going to Happen?" *Huffington Post.* 29 Feb. 2012. Accessed 8 Mar. 2012 <www.huffingtonpost.com.>

[8] Vijayan, Jaikumar. "36 State AGs Blast Google's Privacy Policy Change." *ComputerWorld.* 24 Feb. 2012. Accessed 8 Mar. 2012 <www.computerworld.com>

[9] Gaudin.

[10] Tsukayama, Hayley. "How to Close Your Google Account." *Washington Post.* 25 Jan. 2012. Accessed 8 Mar. 2012 <www.washingtonpost.com>.

[11] Williams, Christopher. "Google Sued for Android Refund Over Privacy Shakeup." *The Telegraph.* 1 Mar. 2012. Accessed 8 Mar. 2012 <www.telegraph.co.uk>.

[12] Ibid.

[13] Vijayan.

[14] Ibid.

[15] Kanter, James. "E.U. Presses Google to Delay Privacy Policy Changes." *The New York Times.* 3 Feb. 2012. Accessed 8 Mar. 2012 <www.nytimes.com>.

[16] Kanter.

[17] Suciu, Peter. "EU Turns up the Volume on Google Privacy Grumbling." *TechNewsWorld.* 1 Mar. 2012. Accessed 8 Mar. 2012 <www.technewsworld.com>.

[18] Ibid.

[19] Ibid.

[20] Gross, Doug. "How to Prepare for Google's Privacy Changes." *CNN.* 29 Feb. 2012. Accessed 8 Mar. 2012 <www.cnn.com>.

[21] Ibid.

[22] Ibid.

[23] "Google Privacy Policy Changes Spark Europe-Wide Inquiry." *The Guardian.* 1 Mar. 2012. Accessed 8 Mar. 2012. <www.guardian.co.uk>.

[24] Ibid.

The Fight to Define U.S. Cybersecurity and Information Sharing Policy

Dan Arnaudo

March 2013

Abstract – *Dan reviews some of the recent political battles over cybersecurity and information sharing policies in the past two years, particularly regarding critical infrastructure. Events covered include failed attempts by Congress to pass the Cyber Intelligence Sharing and Protection (CISPA), the Cybersecurity Acts of 2012, and President Obama's executive order for improving critical infrastructure cybersecurity. Dan identifies and reviews the key objectives of the bills, the debates over them, and the interested stakeholders in the process.*

"America must also face the rapidly growing threat from cyber-attacks. We know hackers steal people's identities and infiltrate private e-mail. We know foreign countries and companies swipe our corporate secrets. Now our enemies are also seeking the ability to sabotage our power grid, our financial institutions, and our air traffic control systems. We cannot look back years from now and wonder why we did nothing in the face of real threats to our security and our economy."

- President Barack Obama, *State of the Union Address*, February 11, 2013[1]

During his 2013 State of the Union Address, U.S. President Barack Obama highlighted the challenges to American cyberspace with this statement. Increasingly, corporations, the government, military and individual citizens have come to rely on the Internet for everything they do, and this has made them uniquely vulnerable to a wide range of threats that emanate online. Government and businesses are increasingly looking for ways to share information related to these problems so that they can become aware of problems as they occur and coordinate better, both when dealing with attacks and preventing them before they occur.

In a much-anticipated action aimed at achieving these ends, President Obama noted in the next lines of the speech that he had just signed an executive order earlier in the day that would attempt to encourage some information sharing along these lines.[2] Many in industry, government and the media predicted this order since Congress failed to pass bills in 2012 that would address cybersecurity and information sharing for online threats and vulnerabilities, particularly for critical infrastructure. However, an executive order is a limited instrument because it lacks the force of legislation and only encourages executive agencies such as the National Institute of Standards and Technology (NIST) to begin to coordinate their own policies. The history of these debates is helpful in understanding the challenges of passing cybersecurity and information sharing policy today. President Obama's executive order is the latest in a series of attempts to balance privacy and security concerns to implement a solution to a problem that is growing rapidly in size, complexity and importance.

In April 2012, partly at the urging of the President and a significant number of private and public sector actors[3], the House of Representatives passed the "Cyber Intelligence Sharing and Protection Act" (CISPA), which would enable the kind of information sharing that President Obama is requesting today.[4] However, the president vowed to veto the act, citing both privacy concerns that the agreement would share too much of the citizens' private information and that it did not do enough to address serious threats to critical infrastructure. In a statement from the Office of Management and Budget, the administration laid out its case:

"The sharing of information must be conducted in a manner that preserves Americans' privacy, data confidentiality, and civil liberties and recognizes the civilian nature of cyberspace. Cybersecurity and privacy are not mutually exclusive. Moreover, information sharing, while an essential component of comprehensive legislation, is not alone enough to protect the Nation's core critical infrastructure from cyber threats."[5]

Organizations such as the Electronic Frontier Foundation (EFF), the American Civil Liberties Union, The Sunlight Foundation, and Reporters Without Borders all opposed the bill on privacy grounds as well. The EFF in particular criticized the bill for being overly broad in terms of information sharing and noted that parties to the agreement would not share information publicly. The bill contained a provision that would make any information shared under its framework irrecoverable by the public through Freedom of Information Act Requests. [6]

Alternatively, the American Chamber of Commerce opposed the bill because it would place overly onerous information sharing demands on U.S. businesses, a position that resonated with many conservatives. The result is that there were challenges from both a public concerned with civil liberties and a private sector concerned with a government overly interested in the affairs of a business, a government that would be enabled to instigate litigation if an enterprise did not share enough information. Obviously, there is a cost to set up any system, including both implementation and then managing compliance to ensure that firms are following the law, a subtext that many commentaries overlooked.

Because of this opposition and the president's veto threat, the bill didn't proceed to the Senate, but elements of it were picked up in when the Senate attempted to pass the Cybersecurity Act of 2012, which incorporated provisions of CISPA but failed on a largely party line vote when it was voted on in August and November.[7] That failure led to the beginning of speculation that President Obama would make an executive order to implement many of its provisions, fulfilled on the day of his State of the Union. Two days after the President's executive order, the cosponsors of CISPA in 2012, Congressmen Mike Rogers (R-MI), chairman of the House Intelligence Committee, and ranking member Dutch Ruppersberger (D-MD), announced that they were reintroducing the measure with some amendments that would limit the scope of the information shared. They also noted in a press conference that they were working with the administration to address privacy concerns and avoid a veto.[8]

The authors' positions point to one of the chief reasons that many detractors of these bills are concerned about privacy, namely that they represent the intelligence community and that institutions like

the National Security Agency will benefit the most
from these kinds of information sharing initiatives,
with little oversight.[9] Intelligence committees in
Congress are supposed to provide this oversight
function but it is unclear to many observers how,
once Congress has vested this power, its members or
the public can really verify what kind of data is being
exchanged.

The concerns raised by members of Congress, the
public, interest groups, and firms the private sector
during the first round of CISPA and the
Cybersecurity Act will continue to be the focus of the
debate over the resurrected bill. Ultimately,
government and industry need to address these issues
and come to some kind of agreement on how they can
coordinate both their information and the policies
that govern them to protect critical infrastructure
better. It is a good thing that this argument is so
vociferous, including the mention during State of the
Union Addresses and discussed by heavyweights in
the public and private sectors participating and
encouraging wider debate. There is a justified urgency
to these calls for political and technical reform.
Whether or not the various parties can come to
agreement on a strong, coherent policy is difficult to
predict, but any decision will form a major
component of how the U.S. will be able to protect its

critical infrastructure such as banking, power and utility systems in future. The security of critical infrastructure is linked inextricably with the privacy and civil rights of its users, and the balancing act to ensure both of these objectives forms the core of the challenge that any sound policy will have to address. However, failure to pass laws regarding cooperation between private and public sectors will have severe consequences for all concerned.

---

[1] Obama, Barack. "Transcript: State of the Union 2013." *ABC News.* 13 Feb. 2013. Accessed 14 Feb. 2013 <www.abcnew.com>

[2] Obama, Barack. "Executive Order -- Improving Critical Infrastructure Cybersecurity." 12 Feb. 2013. Whitehouse. Accessed 15 Feb. 2013. <www.whitehouse.gov>.

[3] "Facebook Backs Cyber-threat Bill." *BBC News.* 16 Apr. 2012. Accessed 15 Feb. 2013 <www.bbc.co.uk>.

[4] "Cyber-Security Bill Past U.S. House." *BBC* News. 27 Apr. 2012. Accessed 15 Feb. 2013 <www.bbc.co.uk>.

[5] Franzen, Carl. "Obama Will Veto CISPA Unless Changes Are Made." *Talking Points Memo.* 25 Apr. 2013. Accessed 15 Feb. 2013 <www.talkingpointsmemo.com>.

[6] Timm, Trevor. "Cybersecurity Bill FAQ: The Disturbing Privacy Dangers in CISPA and How To Stop It." *Electronic Frontier Foundation* 15 Apr. 2012. Accessed 15 Feb. 2013 <www.eff.org>.

[7] Smith, Josh. "Cybersecurity Bill Fails To Advance in Senate, Again." *National Journal* 14 Nov. 2012. Accessed 15 Feb. 2013 <www.nationaljournal.com>.

[8] Franzen, Carl. "Controversial Cyber Bill CISPA Returns to Congress for Debate, Same as Before." *The Verge* 13 Feb. 2013. Accessed 15 Feb. 2013 <www.theverge.com>.

[9] Schwartz, Matthew. "CISPA Bill: 5 Main Privacy Worries." *Information Week* 17 Apr. 2013. Accessed 16 Feb. 2013 <www.informationweek.com>.

The Cyber Intelligence Sharing and Protection Act and Online Privacy

Travis Warren
March 2013

Abstract: *Looking at the issue of protecting privacy and security from a different angle, Travis makes the arguments for the passage of the Cyber Intelligence Sharing and Protection Act (CISPA). He elaborates on the criticisms made by privacy advocates concerning the more controversial aspects of the bill, and looks at the existing solutions currently on the table. Travis also examines the emerging market for cyber weapons, and puts them forward as an alternative area for potential regulation.*

Introduction

Online privacy was, is, and will continue to be a hotly debated topic. This debate continues despite the fact that many CEOs of large technology sector companies have derided the idea of online privacy and gone so far as to declare "the age of privacy to be over."[1] However, public outcry over recent changes to Instagram and Facebook's privacy terms[2] seems to indicate that privacy - and the contractual language supporting privacy protection - do still matter to a large portion of the online community. This is particularly in evidence during the backlashes that inevitably occur in reaction to attempts by the U.S. government to control, regulate, and gain access to personal information of Internet users.

On April 26, 2012, the U.S. House of Representatives passed H.R. 3523 also known as the Cyber Intelligence Sharing and Protection Act (CISPA).[3] CISPA was broadly criticized across the political spectrum with groups as diverse as the American Civil Liberties Union (ACLU)[4] and Freedom Works[5] publicly advocating against its passage. Ultimately, although the bill passed the House, it failed to make its way out of the Senate.[6] Even had the Senate approved the bill, President Obama threatened a veto because CISPA lacked "privacy, confidentiality, and civil liberties safeguards."[7] Despite this, the original sponsors of CISPA are reported to be reintroducing a very similar bill in the 2013 legislative session.[8]

Why CISPA?

At the beginning of its previous stint through the House of Representatives, CISPA was introduced on the House floor by Intelligence Committee Chairman Mike Rogers and was defended as necessary owing to the myriad of threats to U.S. infrastructure and business interests that exist in cyberspace. During the speech, Representative Rogers made three references to China, specifically pointing to the Chinese role in stealing American intellectual property and the resulting cost of American jobs.[9] Charged language and specific countries are referenced in the speech, beginning with this initial statement: "In just the last few years, nation states like China have stolen enough intellectual property from just defense contractors, that would be equivalent to 50 times the print collection of the U.S. Library of Congress"[10]. No specific incidents or data thefts are referenced to defend this assertion and CISPA is put forward as a reasonable counteragent against the specter of foreign enemies without examples as to why this is the case.

Specifics aside, where China is concerned the security community and numerous American journalists share a common or sympathetic view with Representative Rogers. Recently, three prominent newspapers - *The New York Times, The Washington Post,* and *The Wall Street Journal* - went public with claims and evidence that they were victims of cyberattacks that likely originated in China.[11] *The New York Times* stated "Chinese hackers had persistently attacked its computers over the past four months since the paper published a story on Premier Wen Jiabao, but sensitive material related to the report was not accessed."[12] These highly publicized attacks were not the first accusations of illegal behavior by Chinese sponsored cyber criminals. In June 2012, Google publicly claimed that "suspected

Chinese hackers tried to steal the passwords of hundreds of Google email account holders, including those of senior U.S. government officials, Chinese activists and journalists."[13]

Additionally, a recent intelligence assessment appears to contextualize these apparently isolated incidents as examples of a widespread issue.[14] *The Washington Post* reported "the National Intelligence Estimate identifies China as the country most aggressively seeking to penetrate the computer systems of American businesses and institutions to gain access to data that could be used for economic gain."[15] Additionally, the assessment "describes a wide range of sectors that have been the focus of hacking over the past five years, including energy, finance, information technology, aerospace and automotive."[16] These examples indicate that the hyperbole and advocacy for new cybersecurity laws and policy are warranted; however, they do not make an equally compelling case as to why CISPA would improve the otherwise bleak security landscape.

Privacy Concerns

Opponents of CISPA argue that while certain threats are real, security policy, law and privacy should not be mutually exclusive concepts. As an example, an open letter to Congress that was drafted by security experts, engineers and various other industry experts stated that the security community "take(s) security very seriously, but we fervently believe that strong computer and network security does not require Internet users to sacrifice their privacy and civil liberties."[17] The argument then is not whether Internet security should be improved or better policed, but instead that the original CISPA bill lacks protections for the very users it is intended to protect.

Specifically, opponents of CISPA cite the fact that the bill was prefaced with the statement "Notwithstanding any other provision of law."[18] This verbiage allows the provisions of CISPA to supersede any previously drafted legislation that may provide for privacy protections or limitations on government access to private or personal information. Additionally, another section grants immunity to private entities for sharing information with agencies of the federal government that would have previously required a warrant.[19] This section would prevent the possibility of legal ramifications for the sharing of network data, similar to what was seen during the AT&T wiretapping scandal in 2006.[20] While the legislation does not explicitly legalize warrantless wiretapping of the variety seen in the AT&T scandal, it does allow private companies such as AT&T to share that same type of data with the government without risk of liability.

Oversight is also addressed and limited within the
language of the CISPA bill. Specifically it states that
any information shared with a federal agency does
not have to conform to the regulations specified in
the Freedom of Information Act (FOIA).[21] Essentially,
this provision prevents members of the public from
evaluating the scope and details of the information
that would be shared by private entities without first
filing a lawsuit against the government.[22] This is
particularly concerning due to the vagueness of the
language, which defines the initiating reasons and the
class of information that can be shared. H.R. 3523
defines cyber threat information as information
pertaining to vulnerabilities, threats, and efforts to
deny or gain access to any system or network of a
government or private entity.[23] According to the
Electronic Frontier Foundation (EFF), this broad
definition could include "things like port scans, DDoS
traffic, and the like. Indeed, merely using a proxy or
anonymization service to let you browse the web
privately could be construed to be a cybersecurity
threat indicator. Using cryptography to protect one's
communications or access systems securely could
similarly be taken as a way to defeat an operational
control."[24]

Existing Private Sector Solutions

Because the security threats to U.S. networks and related infrastructure are real and documented and that previous attempts at legislating a solution (like CISPA) have failed to provide privacy protections ample enough to inspire passage, the debate then becomes about what the private sector is currently doing to protect its own vulnerable networks. What best practices, guidelines, and markets are filling the void left by the Senate's failure to pass CISPA?

A recent series on National Public Radio (NPR) outlined the major approaches currently being recommended and adopted by the private sector in response to consistent and ongoing cyber threats. The report indicated that the consensus among cybersecurity firms is that the private sector should shift focus from network defenses to a more offense-based strategy.[25] Honeypots are the specific offensive option used to exemplify the potential efficacy of this methodology. A honeypot is a scheme wherein a company plants inaccurate and misleading documentation on its network with the hopes that an attacker would illegally obtain that documentation and the sponsoring agency of that attacker would then act on the false information, ultimately leaving the attacking organization worse off than they were previously. While no other offensive strategies are specified, it is noted that there "is nevertheless a vigorous debate over the legal issues in offensive cyber-operations by private companies."[26] Whatever ethical concerns are raised by the practice of offense as a form of defense, it seems that absent clear legal definition around what is and is not permissible, private companies are likely to start trending in the direction recommended by security experts.

Another extralegal private sector solution discussed in multiple separate reports on NPR[27] and the MIT Technology Review[28] is the role that exploit markets currently play in the economies of network and information security. According to the report, "There is no regulation of the vulnerability market in the U.S."[29] However, the industry exists, and while industry participants prefer to remain somewhat anonymous, the report did state, "in the U.S., the National Security Agency and other branches of the U.S. military, law enforcement and intelligence agencies are among the biggest buyers of vulnerabilities."[30] As the reality of the U.S. government's interest in this market is not accompanied by a large number of reported incidents of federal involvement in the patching of vulnerabilities, it can be assumed that the various agencies involved in these purchases are involved for the offensive capabilities associated with the information.

Conclusion

In reaction to a deteriorating security situation where the cyber weapons market is likely fueling an arms race, President Obama drafted an Executive Order on February 12, 2013 titled "Improving Critical Infrastructure Cybersecurity."[31] The order defines what may be considered critical infrastructure and mandates the creation of a framework for improving security and reducing risks to those structures that meet the definition. Additionally, it outlines a series of policy goals, including the creation of regular threat reports, which will be made available to the private sector and the process by which classified threat information can be released to private companies.[32] The fact that at least some of this classified information is likely to include vulnerabilities purchased on the open market and available to the highest bidders will raise interesting questions regarding the efficacy of the information sharing framework. Should the bar for accessing threat information exceed the expense of purchasing the information on the open market, will private entities choose the exploits market over the framework offered by the government?

Regardless, the Obama administrations' effort to protect critical infrastructure has the potential to be a limited test case in regards to the efficacy of information sharing in combating cyber threats, whereas the reintroduction of CISPA refocuses the cybersecurity discussion on issues that now have legal remedies. With the introduction of the Executive Order on Improving Critical Infrastructure Cybersecurity, at least a portion of the information-sharing intended through CISPA can now be realized. Additionally, it is already illegal to access government or private networks without permission. While reporting these crimes might create negative PR for the company that has been victimized, it would create the opposite direction information-sharing situation that is not defined in the Executive Order. If the government seeks information in an ongoing investigation, it has the legal ability to request a warrant or a national security letter.[33] The merits of speeding up this process or eliminating it all together can be debated but even a completely open information-sharing framework will not help to solve the current escalation of cyberattacks and online criminality.

The threats to U.S. networks and private businesses are very real and the federal government has not taken sufficient steps to regulate the industry that creates, sells, and improves the weapons that are being used to perpetrate these attacks. Quite the contrary, the U.S. government is a known innovator of cyber weaponry[34] and widely recognized as a major customer of the cyber exploits and malware industry.[35] The fact that U.S. agencies are such willing participants in a marketplace that facilitates the very thing being decried in the 2013 State of the Union address[36] makes legislation like CISPA, which require further sacrifices to civil liberties (privacy), seem disingenuous. A more logical first step would be to strengthen the laws combatting the creation and sale of the very weapons the U.S. is attempting to protect its critical infrastructure from; instead of further weakening the legal protections that exist for the population it is the government's job to defend. Further, standing idly by and allowing the exploits industry to flourish likely emboldens and increases the capabilities of nations like China, who's activities are held up as the reason CISPA is required in the first place.

---

[1] Schneier, B. "Google And Facebook's Privacy Illusion." 5 Apr. 2010. *Forbes.* Accessed 15 Feb. 2013 <www.forbes.com>.

[2] Timberg, C. "Instagram, Facebook Stir Online Protests With Privacy Policy Change." *Washington Post.* 18 Dec. 2012. Accessed <www.washingtonpost.com>.

[3] Rogers, M. *Cyber Intelligence Sharing and Protection Act.* 7 May 2012. Accessed <www.gpo.gov>.

[4] *ACLU Opposition to H.R. 3523, the Cyber Intelligence Sharing and Protection Act of 2011.* American Civil Liberties Union. 1 Dec. 2011. Accessed 15 Feb. 2013 <www.aclu.org>.

[5] Borowski, J. "House Passes Online Privacy Invasive CISPA". 17 Apr. 2012. *Freedom Works.* Accessed 15 Feb. 2013 <www.freedomworks.org>.

[6] Martinez, J. "Cybersecurity Act Fails Senate Vote." 2 Aug. 2012. *The Hill.* Accessed 15 Feb. 2013 <www.thehill.com>

[7] *Statement of Administration Policy - H.R. 3523 - Cyber Intelligence Sharing and Protection Act.* The White House 25 Apr. 2012. Accessed 15 Feb 2013 <www.whitehouse.gov>.

[8] *Protecting the American Economy from Cyber Attacks: Introducing the "Cyber Intelligence Sharing and Protection Act of 2013.* 13 Feb. 2013. The Permanent Select Committee on Intelligence Democratic Office. Accessed 15 Feb. 2013, <democrats.intelligence.house.gov>.

[9] Rogers, M. *Chairman Mike Rogers Statement.* The Permanent Select Committee on Intelligence. 26 Apr. 2013. Accessed 15 Feb. 2013 <intelligence.house.gov>.

[10] ibid.

[11] Blanchard, B. "New York Times Says Targeted By China Hackers After Wen Report." *Reuters.* 31 Jan. 2013. Accessed 15 Feb. 2013 <www.reuters.com>.

[12] Ibid.

[13] Wee, S. -L. "Google Reveals Gmail Hacking, Says Likely From China." *Reuters.* 2 Jun. 2011. Accessed 15 Feb. 2013 <www.reuters.com>

[14] Nakashima, E. "U.S. Said To Be Target Of Massive Cyber-Espionage Campaign." *The Washington Post.* 10 Feb. 2013. Accessed 15 Feb. 2013 <www.washingtonpost.com>.

[15] Ibid.

[16] Ibid.

[17] *An Open Letter From Security Experts, Academics and Engineers to the U.S. Congress: Stop Bad Cybersecurity Bills.* Electronic Frontier Foundation. 23 Apr. 2012. Accessed 15 Feb. 2013 <www.eff.org>.

[18] McCullagh, D. "How CISPA Would Affect You (FAQ)." *CNET News.* 27 Apr. 2012. Accessed 15 Feb. 2013 <news.cnet.com>.

[19] Ibid.

[20] Singel, R. "AT&T Sued Over NSA Eavesdropping." *Wired*. 31 Jan. 2006.
Accessed 15 Feb. 2013 <www.wired.com>.

[21] Jaycox, M. M. "CISPA, the Privacy-Invading Cybersecurity Spying Bill, is Back
in Congress." Electronic Frontier Foundation. 13 Feb. 2013. Accessed
15 Feb. 2013 < www.eff.org>.

[22] Ibid.

[23] McCullagh.

[24] Ibid.

[25] Gjelten, T. "Victims Of Cyberattacks Get Proactive Against Intruders."
National Public Radio. 13 Feb. 2013. Accessed 15 Feb. 2013
<www.npr.org>.

[26] Ibid.

[27] Gjelten, T. "In Cyberwar, Software Flaws Are A Hot Commodity." *National
Public Radio*. 12 Feb. 2013. Accessed 15 Feb. 2013 <www.npr.org>.

[28] Simonite, T. "Welcome to the Malware-Industrial Complex." *MIT Technology
Review*. 13 Feb. 2013. Accessed 15 Feb. 2013
<www.technologyreview.com>.

[29] Ibid.

[30] Ibid.

[31] *Executive Order -- Improving Critical Infrastructure Cybersecurity*. The White
House. 12 Feb. 2013. Accessed Feb. 16, 2013 <www.whitehouse.gov>.

[32] Ibid.

[33] "National Security Letters." American Civil Liberties Union. n.d. Accessed
Feb. 16, 2013 <www.aclu.org>.

[34] Williams, C. "Stuxnet Virus: U.S. Refuses to Deny Involvement." *The
Telegraph*. 27 May 2011. Accessed Feb. 16, 2013
<www.telegraph.co.uk>.

[35] Simonite.

[36] *Transcript of President Obama's 2013 State of the Union*. San Jose Mercury
News. 12 Feb. 2013. Accessed 15 Feb. 2013
<www.mercurynews.com>.

The Foreign Intelligence Surveillance Act of 1978: A Review of FISA, the FISC, Current Controversies and Criticisms

Suzann Q. Parker

April 2013

Abstract: *Suzann provides a detailed review of the history of the Foreign Intelligence Surveillance Act of 1978, from the foundations of enactment to amendments and recent debates. She also examines how it reflects the system of checks and balances between the three branches of government. Ultimately, Suzann looks at the fundamental conflict facing governments – finding the balance between protecting the safety of a nation and protecting the rights of its citizens.*

Bill of Rights

"The right of the people to be secure in their persons, houses, papers, and effects, against unreasonable searches and seizures, shall not be violated, and no Warrants shall issue, but upon probable cause, supported by Oath or affirmation, and particularly describing the place to be searched, and the persons or things to be seized."[1]

Far back in recorded history, there are indicators that citizens of states have fought for a certain level of privacy and protection of seizure from their own governments. The Romans had protections against soldiers entering their homes and seizing wealth. The English had protection against the king's guard. Citizenry too has expectations and a need to be protected from aggressions from outside states (aka national security). In society, there has always been a tension between the state and their use of military/policing forces and the desires of the citizens of that society to live their lives in peace and without fear. English common law says that a man's home is his castle. This idea that as a citizen in a society, you have sovereignty in the privacy of your home is the backbone of the fourth Amendment of the Bill of Rights of the U.S.

Thomas Jefferson lobbied strongly for the inclusion of a bill of rights in the constitution. In his letters to James Madison he stated, "A bill of rights is what the people are entitled to against every government on earth, general or particular, and what no just government should refuse, or rest on inference."[2] Anti-federalists eventually agreed to and signed the Constitution, with the stipulation of the development of a series of amendments to be made to the Constitution in the form of a Bill of Rights.

The rationale that governments use to perform surveillance, search, and seizure on their citizens is that of national security. In the U.S., this happened many times throughout our history, from the Revolutionary War to the Vietnam Era to the Cold War and in recent times, the War on Terror. During times of crisis of national security, powers of the executive branch are expanded, allowing greater freedoms of intelligence agencies to perform surveillance. Liberties are taken and citizens' rights are violated. The three branches of government in the U.S. offer our citizens a balance of power, and process of error correction in the running of the country. The judicial branch hears cases of these violations and their findings becoming law that limits executive power. The legislative branch may make modifications and amendments to the law through lobbying, debate, and vote. However, the President must approve them. This process of self-correction has occurred many times since the Bill of Rights and can be seen in the history of the enactment and amendments to the Foreign Intelligence Surveillance Act of 1978.

The Foreign Intelligence Surveillance Act of 1978 (FISA)

FISA was enacted under the backdrop of the fallout from Vietnam and the Watergate scandal. Warrantless surveillance of U.S. Citizens on U.S. soil came to light and spawned committees and hearings in congress. Senator Frank Church was particularly influential, his findings citing "substantial wrongdoing and that intelligence activities had not generally been governed and controlled in accord with the fundamental principles of the U.S. Constitution."[3] The purpose of FISA was to provide protections for U.S. citizen's fourth amendment rights through definitions, procedure, checks and balances in the application of foreign intelligence surveillance. It required warrants, proof of probable cause, and that the primary purpose of the surveillance is to obtain foreign intelligence information. FISA requires that minimization efforts be in place in the investigative procedures to protect citizens. The act also established the U.S. Foreign Intelligence Surveillance Court (FISC) and the Foreign Intelligence Surveillance Court of Review, for authorizing warrants under FISA. Before that time, the President could authorize warrantless surveillance, with no checks and balances for protecting a citizen's rights.

Probable cause in a criminal investigation requires sufficient evidence of a crime being committed or being planned. FISA separated the collection of foreign intelligence from criminal investigation and prosecution. Non-criminal (electronic) surveillance was now only legal for gathering foreign intelligence. Probable cause under FISA was that of ensuring that the target of investigation was a foreign power or agent of a foreign power – not that there was proof of a threat of war or terrorism.

FISA in Context of Checks and Balances

In the last 35 years of FISA, technology has grown leaps and bounds and the focus of national security concerns have morphed many times over. FISA has been amended to meet these new challenges. See Appendix: An Annotated Timeline of FISA, for an overview. In 1994 for example, FISA was amended to provide the ability to apply for physical search and seizure warrant (FISA originally only covered electronic surveillance). This was in reaction to the investigation of Aldrich Ames, a U.S. Citizen, CIA agent, and Soviet spy. President Bill Clinton authorized physical search and seizure under the provision of FISA that circumvents application for warrant – it was authorized under signature of then Attorney General Janet Reno, causing a controversy and challenges from Aldrich Ames' lawyer.[4] This incident demonstrated the need to consider physical evidence in the gathering of national intelligence and the legislature took it up and passed it. A primary argument was that citizen's rights would be better protected if physical searches related to foreign intelligence are authorized under warrant by the

FISC, rather than by the Attorney General, through executive order.

The USA PATRIOT Act, enacted in 2001, reflected extreme change in intelligence gathering practices and concern for national security after the September 11, 2001 terrorist attacks on U.S. soil. The political fallout from this incident focused highly on what went wrong with the foreign intelligence programs. Many changes and expansions were added to FISA. Electronic surveillance definitions were expanded to include the tracking of Internet communications. Protocols were put in place to require intelligence agencies to share information and to collaborate on surveillance and investigations.[5] It also changed the definition of the purpose of investigation from the "primary" reason for gathering foreign intelligence to being a "significant" reason. This weakened the wall between criminal and foreign intelligence investigations. The use of National Security Letters to order businesses to hand over customer records was expanded. A greater number of officials were provided the ability to authorize NSLs, and the type of information was expanded from just financial to communications and other business records. A gag order was required, so those that were served an NSL could not disclose any part of it or their participation in it – even to their lawyers. Most surprisingly was the lifting of the requirement that NSLs pertain solely to foreign powers or agents of foreign powers; the information just had to be relevant to an investigation. NSLs were not subject to judicial review, nor penalties for improper disclosure.[6]

In 2006, three key amendments were made to the PATRIOT Act to reign back in the executive branch's power to perform sweeping investigations that violated U.S. citizens' right to privacy. First, business records were added as a surveillance category under FISA. Surveillance of this type must now meet probable cause warrant requirements and is subject to judicial oversight of the FISC. This action reflected legislative and judicial branches re-balancing power, greatly inspired by the revelation the year before that the NSA was performing wholesale wiretapping of U.S. citizens without warrants through compelling telecommunications companies to share their data. The act still contained the gag order provision, which was later modified through court order (judicial balance of power), finding that it violated free-speech rights by prohibiting businesses from consulting legal counsel.[7]

The 2006 amendment also included the Lone-Wolf provision which allowed a definition of a potential target to be a lone-wolf actor – not directly linked as an agent of a foreign power, but as one participating in terrorist activities. Adding this definition to the act certainly expanded FISA, but it also shifted this intelligence surveillance under judicial oversight; rather than being performed using executive order and national security letter. It ensured that these investigations were under the scrutiny of judicial review, and that guidelines for probable cause were being met (as defined for a lone-wolf actor).

Finally, in the 2006 act, additional enhancements were made to require the Attorney General to submit annual reports to the House and Senate Judiciary Committees on investigations authorized by the FISC. There were additional provisions to require information about electronic surveillance on citizens to be reported every six months. This marked the first time that the executive branch was required to report information out to the legislative branch, with the intent of improving congressional oversight.

The Protect America Act of 2007 brought yet more change that expanded the executive branch's power. It enabled warrant-less electronic surveillance, whether or not U.S. Citizens were the target, with no limits and immunity from prosecution for providers who assist the government. It enabled the President of the U.S. to authorize, for 1 year, warrant-less non-electronic surveillance, with the foreign target limitations. The act required that the Attorney

General certify that these conditions are met under seal to the FISC and to report compliance to the House Permanent Select Committee on Intelligence and Senate Select Committee on Intelligence.[8] The act limited judicial oversight of intelligence gathering in particular. It limited the FISC involvement to reviewing statements after activities had already occurred, and removed all oversight over electronic surveillance. These changes caused immediate debate and outcry, not just from organizations like the ACLU, but also bi-partisan groups such as the Constitution Project's Liberty and Security Committee. "We… are deeply concerned that many of the amendments to the Foreign Intelligence Surveillance Act (FISA) contained in the recently enacted Protect America Act (Pub. L. 110-55) are unnecessarily overbroad, undermine our constitutional system of checks and balances, and fail to sufficiently protect the privacy of the communications of Americans."[9]

The FISA Amendments Act of 2008 made some inroads to rebalance these changes by reinstating the original definition of electronic surveillance. This ensured electronic surveillance is subject to the same burden of proof of foreign targets for gathering foreign intelligence. It provided retroactive and future immunity from prosecution for complying with government agencies' surveillance orders - even if that surveillance was illegal. This protected telecommunications companies for complying with government orders. The act also provided provisions to tighten up the PATRIOT Act and Protect America Act to curtail the government's ability to search U.S. citizens, and placed additional checks and balances - requiring greater approvals by the FISC and annual reports on the Presidential Surveillance Program. It also prohibited the government from invoking war powers or other authorities to supersede surveillance rules in the future.[10]

The Debate Continues

After much debate on unsuccessful amendments to further require transparency of surveillance performed under FISA, the FISA Amendments Act was recently renewed until 2017 without change.[11] Debate continues in the U.S. Senate on the existence of "Secret Law" in the FISC. FISC rulings and opinions on cases are not declassified, nor summarized and released to the public. Therefore, there is a lot of opinion and interpretation of the laws by the FISC that is unknown to the people. While members of the Senate continue to debate this, the Supreme Court has just made an important ruling (Amnesty v. Clapper) that warrantless wiretapping could not be challenged in court, because the plaintiff lacked the standing to do so – in that they could not prove that they had been subject to surveillance. This of course is not possible to know by ordinary citizens, as this information is classified.[12]

Suggestions by many are for the Attorney General to release un-classified versions of the rulings of the FISC. Efforts are also being made to pressure the Attorney General to release more statistics about the number of U.S. citizens that are incidentally targets of surveillance.[13] Members of Senate Intelligence Committee debated against this, claiming that there are classified reasons why releasing this data would cause national security problems.

In addition to the transparency questions, there are also many still debated modernization questions related to FISA. Since the USA PATRIOT Act redefined electronic surveillance to include Internet traffic and communications – there have been several efforts made to adapt the law to changing technology. The 2006 PATRIOT Act amendment provided for "Roving wiretaps" – which are not agents driving around in vans, but are wiretaps that are authorized to follow the target of surveillance, not to be specifically linked to the phone or IP address. This was enacted to address the issue of the use of disposable phones and simply moving locations to avoid detection.[14] FISA does not address data-mining,

surveillance drones, and many yet to be thought of
ways of gathering data under the auspices of national
security. The debates will likely continue over the
years to come.

Reflection

In context, FISA and how and why it has morphed
over the years demonstrates the give and take that our
nation must make in order to both protect the safety
of its citizens and to protect their rights under the
constitution. The Constitution and Bill of Rights were
put in place to ensure that our basic rights were
protected – the rights that we as a nation agreed to
build our society on. Those laws are at the core of all
our other laws and our three branches of government
are set up to ensure that a balance is struck between
competing interests. The world is always changing,
but our system is built to rebalance us and put us back
on the right track as a nation. It provides hope that
some elements of the current incarnation of FISA that
overstretch will eventually come back into balance. It
also points out that we as citizens have a continuing
responsibility to communicate to our elected
representatives to encourage them to protect our
rights and to fight for transparency.

Appendix: An Annotated Timeline of FISA

Event	Year	Context

Semayne's Case	1604	Important early case in England that illustrates the common law - A man's house is his castle,[15] a precedent of the 4th Amendment. Sir Edward Coke's opinion stated, "The house of every one is to him as his castle and fortress, as well for his defense against injury and violence as for his repose."[16]
Ratification of the Bill of Rights	1791	The Bill of Rights is ratified, including the 4th Amendment: "The right of the people to be secure in their persons, houses, papers, and effects, against unreasonable searches and seizures, shall not be violated, and no Warrants shall issue, but upon probable cause, supported by Oath or affirmation, and particularly describing the place to be searched, and the persons or things to be seized."[17]
Christopher Pyle	1970	Christopher Pyle uncovered evidence that the U.S. Army Intelligence Command had over 1,500 officers in the U.S. commissioned to spy on any known protests or demonstrations with more than 20 participants.[18] Senator Sam Ervin (D-NC) and

		Senator Frank Church (D-ID) launched committee investigations into warrant-less government surveillance of civilians.[19]
Watergate Scandal Broke	1973	The 1972 break-in at the Democratic National Committee headquarters brought to light. Includes convictions on attempted wiretapping.
Warrant-less CIA Surveillance	1974	Seymour Hersh publishes report about large-scale warrant-less CIA surveillance. Church committee findings cited "substantial wrongdoing and that intelligence activities had not generally been governed and controlled in accord with the fundamental principles of the U.S. Constitution."[20]
Foreign Intelligence Surveillance Act	1978	Senator Ted Kennedy brings to floor FISA, Carter signs it - Law intended to protect U.S. Citizens against unreasonable search and seizure in the act of gathering foreign intelligence. Requires a warrant to be judicially sanctioned and supported by probable cause. Foreign Intelligence Surveillance Court formed to preside over classified, ex parte proceedings.

Aldrich Ames Controversy	1994	Aldrich Ames, a convicted soviet spy brought to light the conflicts with physical search and seizure and criminal law. Congress added amendment to FISA to enable the FISC to authorize physical search warrants.[21]
USA PATRIOT Act	2001	As a response to the September 11, 2001 attacks on the U.S., the act made sweeping changes that expanded the executive branch's scope for surveillance for foreign intelligence purposes. For example, internet communications was added under Pen Register and Trap and Trace surveillance. The burden of proof was relaxed - no longer requiring that the surveillance must be for foreign intelligence purposes. It also weakened the wall between criminal investigations and national security investigations - requiring agencies to share intelligence across agencies (invalidating the exclusionary rule), and it removed the requirement to provide proof that a target is a non-citizen and foreign agent.[22]

NSA Illegal Warrant-less Wiretapping	2005	Warrant-less wiretapping by the National Security Agency (NSA) was revealed publicly in late 2005 by The New York Times. Multiple telecoms were implicated in being complicit with the wholesale collection of communication data and content.[23]
PATRIOT Act Renewed	2006	Additional amendments were added to include the search of business records - providing the government with the authority to compel businesses such as cell carriers, to hand over data. This included a gag order - prohibiting those businesses from informing their customers of the government's activities. Later court cases altered this allow warrant recipients to tell their own lawyers/counsel. Includes lone-wolf provisions.[24]
Protect America Act	2007	The Protect America Act enables the President of the U.S. authorize, for 1 year, warrant-less surveillance on: "groups engaged in international terrorism or activities in preparation therefore; foreign-based political organizations, not substantially

		composed of U.S. persons; or entities that are directed and controlled by a foreign government or governments." The act requires that the Attorney General certify that these conditions are met under seal to the FISC and to report compliance to the House Permanent Select Committee on Intelligence and Senate Select Committee on Intelligence. The act changed the definition of electronic surveillance, it is no longer classifed as having to proclude U.S. citizens, and is not required to be authorized under warrant.[25]
FISA Amendments Act	2008	The FISA Amendments Act reinstated definition of electronic surveillance as being on foreign individuals, provided retroactive and future immunity from prosecution for complying with government agencies' surveillance orders - even if that surveillance was illegal. Provided provisions to tighten up the PATRIOT Act and Protect America Act to curtail the government's ability to search U.S. citizens, and placed additional checks and balances - requiring

		greater approvals by the FISC and annual reports on the Presidential Surveillance Program. It also prohibited the government from invoking war powers or other authorities to supersede surveillance rules in the future.[26]
FISA Amendments Act Renewed	2012	After much debate on unsuccessful amendments to further require transparency of surveillance performed under FISA, the FISA Amendments Act was renewed until 2017 without change. Debate continues in the senate on the existence of "Secret Law" in the FISC, because their opinions on cases are not declassified, nor summarized and released to the public. Therefore, there is a lot of opinion and interpretation of the laws that is unknown to the people. Efforts are also being made to pressure the Attorney General to release more statics about the number of U.S. citizens that are incidentally targets of surveillance.[27]

---

[1] *U.S. Constitution.* Amend. IV.

[2] Jefferson, Thomas. "Thomas Jefferson to James Madison." *The Thomas Jefferson Papers Series 1. General Correspondence. 1651-1827.* 1787. 727. Library of Congress. Accessed Apr. 2013 <www.loc.gov>.

[3] Stolz, B. A. "The Foreign Intelligence Surveillance Act of 1978: The Role of Symbolic Politics." *Law & Policy.* 2002.

[4] York, Byron. "Clinton Claimed Authority to Order No-Warrant Searches." *National Review Online.* 20 Dec. 2005. Accessed Apr. 2013 <www.nationalreview.com>.

[5] Ashcroft, John. "Memorandum: Intelligence Sharing Procedures for Foreign Intelligence and Foreign Counterintelligence Investigations Conducted by the FBI." Office of the Director of National Intelligence. 6 Mar. 2002. Accessed Apr. 2013 <www.dni.gov>.

[6] Doyle, Charles. "National Security Letters in Foreign Intelligence Investigations: A Glimpse of the Legal Background and Recent Amendments." Congrssional Research Service Report. 21 Mar. 2006. Accessed Apr. 2013 <www.fpc.state.gov>.

[7] "USA PATRIOT Improvement and Reauthorization Act of 2005." Federation of American Scientists. 2005. Accessed Apr. 2013 <www.fas.org>.

[8] "Protect America Act of 2007." *P. L. 110-55.* 2007. Accessed Apr. 2013 <www.gpo.gov>.

[9] Constitution Project's Liberty and Security Committee. *Statement on the Protect America Act.* Washington, DC: The Constitution Project, 2007. Accessed Apr. 2013 <www.constitutionproject.org>.

[10] *Foreign Intelligence Surveillance Act of 1978 Amendments Act Of 2008.* U.S. Senate Select Committee on Intelligence. 10 Jul. 2008. Accessed Apr. 2013 <www.intelligence.senate.gov>.

[11] Chappell, Bill. "President And Congress Extend FISA Wiretapping Act To 2017 [Updated]." 28 Dec. 2012. *National Public Radio.* Accessed Apr. 2013 <www.npr.org>.

[12] Serwer, Adam. "Supreme Court: You Can't Challenge Secret Law Because It's Secret." *Mother Jones* 27 Feb. 2013. Accessed Apr. 2013 <www.motherjones.com>.

[13] Chappell.

[14] "USA PATRIOT"

[15] Cuddihy, William and B. Carmon Hardy. "A Man's House Was Not His
        Castle: Origins of the Fourth Amendment to the U.S. Constitution."
        The William and Mary Quarterly. 1980.

[16] Szabo, Nick. "Seyman's Case." *Nick Szabo's Essays, Papers, and Concise
        Tutorials. n.d.* Accessed Apr. 2013 <www.szabo.best.vwh.net>.

[17] *U.S. Conststitution.*

[18] Pyle, Christopher H. "CONUS Intelligence: The Army Watches Civilian
        Politics ; And, the Army Covers Up." *Washington Monthly.* 1970.

[19] Stolz.

[20] Stolz.

[21] York.

[22] "Ammendments to the Foreign Intelligence Surveillance Act (FISA)."
        Federation of American Scientists. n.d. Accessed Apr. 2013
        <www.fas.org>.

[23] Risen, James and Eric Lichtblau. "Bush Lets U.S. Spy on Callers Without
        Courts." *The New York Times* 16 Dec. 2005. Accessed Apr. 2013
        <www.nytimes.com>.

[24] "USA PATRIOT Improvement and Reauthorization Act of 2005."

[25] "Protect America Act of 2007."

[26] *Foreign Intelligence Surveillance Act.*

[27] Chappell.

Risks in Digital Identity After Death

Jess Mauer

July 2013

Abstract: *People have been transitioning remnants of their identity from conventional physical effects, such as photos and trinkets, to online profiles and social networks. Identity is being digitalized and with this, complications arise as the population ages. Jess explores how a death today presents more complex issues than before the digital age. The component of an online identity does not fit in the mold of our society's traditional framework for dealing with death. Jess presents the new risks regarding the ethics, legality, and privacy of an individual's digital identity after their death.*

Introduction

People have been grappling with digital identity issues since objects have expanded into digital space, rather than just the physical world. People crossed a threshold some time ago, where it became easier to create things online rather than to purge them. The results are overflowing inboxes, camera rolls, and status updates. Now that we can store thousands of photos on our smart phones and with Facebook reporting a billion active users last year,[1] there's no need to be discerning when deciding what objects of your past to keep; you can keep everything, and keep it online — a concept that the general public has accepted with such relish that seeing a photo album in someone's home almost feels quaint.

Amassed over a lifetime, these digital photos, emails, and status updates paint a story of someone's identity in a way that a shoebox of trinkets used to. However, identity is different when it is digital. Physical remnants do not have controls provided to online accounts and can be contained in one location. In addition, because they are physical things, they have to be purged. An individual must make concerted decisions about what to keep and what to get rid of. On the Internet, these "trinkets" could be strewn among a multitude of different sites, amassed in huge quantities.

As this data is collected and cultivated in an online space, it develops into a user's identity, access to which is locked behind a password. This becomes a complicated problem when the user passes away. After a loved one dies, a troubling but natural process for survivors is to go through the deceased's remaining possessions for memorial and closure. This process becomes drastically altered if everything is password protected and inaccessible.

A simple solution might be disclose your password to a trusted source in the event of your death, which begins a slippery risk slope of gray areas. First, facing one's own mortality is a commonly avoided topic. Most Americans do not even have a will, so it is no surprise that planning for what would happen to their digital identity after death is not on most individuals' radar (a quick Internet search found from 30 to 50 percent are will-less, but I couldn't find a specific verifiable source on this). If someone were to pass away unexpectedly, a surprisingly lot more is lost to their loved ones if they do not know the passwords or do not even know where to look online.

Those who are attempting to develop an appropriate framework for this problem are floating ideas like having an "authorized user" attached to social network accounts or sharing their passwords with a trusted source.[2] However, the legality of this is unclear, as will be discussed later in this research note. Moreover, not every user is willing to have this kind of disclosure. The uneasiness of thinking about death combined with the uneasiness of sharing access to a "private" space makes it easy to see why people do not want to deal with this emerging problem.

Just like anything else that people typically do not enjoy doing, there are options to pay for a solution to maintain your digital identities securely for your beneficiaries. A few of the main options are sites like Legacy Locker and Asset Lock. Both sites allow you to assign a beneficiary and recommend you use their space as a one-stop digital backup for all your valuable documents (deeds, trusts, etc.). Thankfully, both sites claim to use 256 bit encryption and SSL. Privacy is another issue. While Legacy Locker states explicitly they will not share user data with 3rd parties for marketing, Asset Lock does disclose that they aggregate user data to 3rd parties — which shouldn't exactly instill comfort in those thinking about linking all their banking, email and social media. Asset Lock does address a risk of future uncertainty in their business by having a policy if they are shut down.[3] A user would not be able to locate an equivalent policy with Legacy Locker.[4]

Then there are sites like Death Switch, which allows users to upload messages to send to specific individuals upon their death. The site recommends using the message service for banking information, funeral plans, computer passwords, love notes, or unspeakable secrets. The user is emailed periodically to verify that they are still living and if an answer is not received, the messages are sent.[5] This seems like a great premise for a summer blockbuster considering the amount of emails that get lost in most inboxes.

Risks

While the startups are figuring a way to profit from this digital identity after death, it is important from the risk assessment perspective to take a closer look at the gray areas involved in these decisions.

Risk #1 – Single Point of Failure

Putting all your digital/personal identity in one location creates a single point of failure and a huge risk to your data privacy, especially considering the type of information they recommend you upload to their servers. Sites like Legacy Locker or Asset Lock could have a breach. They could fail as a business and shut down. Or with no transparency in this space, they could lie about how and for what they are using your data. These businesses have not been around long enough to gain user trust. Storing your data over a lifetime is a long time when the average online startups fail 30 to 40 percent of the time.6 This risk is high for the user — having this data lost or compromised would be detrimental on their online identity.

Risk #2 – It's Probably Illegal

It is definitely against the terms of service of many of the popular social and electronic communication sites. Whether someone might disclose login information to one of the digital afterlife businesses or to a significant other, they are still disclosing something they agree not to do when signing up for these sites. Here are a few examples:

- *Facebook*: "You will not share your password, let anyone else access your account, or do anything else that might jeopardize the security of your account."[7]
- *Yahoo*: "You are responsible for maintaining the confidentiality of the password and account and are fully responsible for all activities that occur under your password or account."[8]
- *LinkedIn*: "You agree to: 1) keep your password secure and confidential; 2) not permitted to others to use your account; 3) not use other's accounts..."[9]

Legally speaking there is not much precedent to follow; however, it is technically against the law, at least according to the Computer Fraud and Abuse Act. This act makes any unauthorized access of an online account a criminal offense.[10] This is also true based on the Stored Communications Act, which was originally created to enhance the rights of privacy extended by the fourth amendment to the digital realm.[11] This is a good thing, but when it is utilized in the context of a user's death, it can be used to bring criminal penalties for unauthorized access of electronic communications and remote computing services. Criminal penalties that could arise from disclosure of your password and login information as the businesses mentioned above require for their business model to function, making it risky to the users and their executors or to the businesses running digital afterlife planning sites.

Many social media sites understand this, which helps to mitigate the risk. Facebook has gone so far as to create an option to put someone's timeline in a "memorial" state, where users can still post messages, photos, and videos. However, no one can log on, only confirmed friends can see the content, and private messages remain private. This is an interesting compromise because it allows those grieving to have a space to come together and share memories and feelings in a way that is very organic to our current generation. However, it does have its limitations. The page of the deceased is locked down in order to prohibit new friends from being confirmed and the private messages from being read.[12]

Sites that do not have a service like this, like a blogging site, remain accessible in their current state, but run into another familiar Internet problem — spambots. Nothing could be more disrespectful to someone's memory than to have their blog filled with spambots with no way to remove them if site login is not possible.

On the other hand, allowing anyone, even an estate executor, to log into any of the decease's online profiles violates the essence of an access-controlled space. This brings up ethical implications regarding how our society should handle the privacy rights of the deceased.

Risk #3 - Privacy Violations of the Deceased User

Would users be willing to use these sites for their intended purposes if they know this information would be released upon their death? What happens if, upon death, a user's privacy is violated by someone who gained access to their online accounts and defamed the deceased's character? Social media sites also need to protect the integrity and authenticity of their product and protect user trust. Any violation of privacy, even to a deceased user, reflects negatively on their business and brand integrity.

States are slowly beginning to create legislation to support people going through this process. Five states have laws on the books for digital estate planning and many more have laws in the works. Connecticut was the first in October 2005 with Public Act No. 05-136. This requires email providers to provide estate executor with a copy of deceased individual's mailbox contents. Other states followed; Rhode Island in May 2007 with HB 5647 and Indiana in July 2007 with Code 29-1-13. It was not until Oklahoma passed

HB2800 in November 2010 that there was any verbiage explicitly stating social networking or the ability to do more than just have a downloaded copy of the content. HB2800 stated that executors had the right to control, continue, or terminate any online accounts of the deceased. Idaho passed a similar law in July 2011 and many more states plan on following.[13]

Conclusion

Response to all three of these risks is a matter of acceptance or sharing. Using a third party site to organize digital assets can be seen as a shared response with the site. However, the most likely risk response is acceptance. While technically possible that any type of password disclosure or "unauthorized access" could receive criminal penalties, this has yet to occur and it seems like our legal system has bigger fish to fry. In addition, as sites like Facebook have shown their "memorial" profiles and states like Connecticut, Rhode Island, Indiana, Oklahoma, and Idaho have put laws on their books, it is clear this issue is increasingly visible. The only risk that remains high is one of privacy. It is hard to say how much access will be allowed in the future, but as more and more states pass laws allowing estate executors access to all online accounts to continue, maintain or terminate them, a pattern is developing. A pattern that does not take into account a method to understand a user's last wishes or who may access their online information after they pass. In death, as in life, there is always a counter balance of privacy and security access. Who has access to your shoebox of trinkets or a safety deposit box is a very personal decision, and the same applies to anything online. It will be interesting to see where on the spectrum the future standard of digital access after death lands.

[1] Crawford, D. "Facebook Reports Fourth Quarter and Full Year 2012 Results." Facebook, Inc. 30 Jan. 2013. Accessed Jun. 2013 <www.investor.faceook.com>.

[2] Walker, R. "Cyberspace When You're Dead." *The New York Times.* 5 Jan. 2011. Accessed Jun. 2013 <www.nytimes.com>.

[3] "Asset Lock Terms of Service." AssetLock. Accessed Jun. 2013 <www.assetlock.net>.

[4] "Legacy Locker Terms of Service." Legacy Locker. 18 Mar. 2009. Accessed Jun. 2013 <legacylocker.com>.

[5] Death Switch Terms of Service." Death Switch. 2006. Accessed Jun. 2013 <www.deathswitch.com>.

[6] Gage, D. "The Venture Capital Secret: 3 Out of 4 Start-Ups Fail." *The Wall Street Journal.* 19 Sep. 2012. Accessed Jun. 2013 <www.wsj.com>.

[7] "Facebook Terms of Service." 11 Dec. 2012. Accessed Jun. 2013 <www.facebook.com>.

[8] "Yahoo! Terms of Service." Yahoo Inc. 16 Mar. 2012. Accessed Jun. 2013 <www.yahoo.com>.

[9] "LinkedIn Terms of Service." LinkedIn Inc. 13 May 2013. Accessed <www.linkedin.com>.

[10] *Prosecuting Computer Crimes.* Office of Legal Education, Executive Office for U.S. Attorneys. 2010. Accessed Jun. 2013 <www.justice.gov>.

---

[11] Kerr, O. S. *A User's Guide to the Stored Communications Act, and a Legislator's Guide to Amending It.* Social Science Research Network. 2004. Accessed Jun. 2013 <www.ssrn.com>

[12] Facebook.

[13] *Law.* Digital Estate Resource. n.d. Accessed Jun. 8, 2013 <www.digitalestateresource.com>.

Chapter III
Finance

Virtual Currency: The Next Generation Banking Model

Devin Luco

May 2013

Abstract – *In recent history, the governments of the world have been tasked with the creation and regulation of currencies. However, the concept of virtual currency is emerging as an interesting concept in its early stages. Devin describes the unique features of virtual currencies, specifically Bitcoin, and discusses the reasons for its consumer attraction and the associated risks.*

What is Virtual Currency?

Virtual currency is an alternate form of money that is non-government created, electronic, and can be used to purchase goods and services from online as well as traditional retailers. One of the most current popular forms of virtual currency is Bitcoin. The concept of Bitcoin was introduced through a 2008 paper written by Satoshi Nakamoto, which proposed a peer-to-peer system that allowed payments to be sent between anonymous online users without the intermediary use of a financial institution.[1] In 2009, Bitcoin went live with the purpose of being a "peer-to-peer electronic cash system" that ensured that the same "coin(s)" was not being spent more than once by a single owner.[2]

This was accomplished with complex math functions as well as publicly recorded time stamped transactions.[3] Once a transaction has occurred, the transaction is irreversible.[4] Despite the efforts of many journalists, very little is known of the developer or group of developers known by the pseudonym, Satoshi Nakamoto. However, in April reports claimed that Satoshi owns at least one million Bitcoins, which at that time's exchange rate was worth approximately $96 million.[5]

Bitcoins are unlike traditional fiat currency. The Bitcoin currency is not issued by a government organization or managed by a central bank.[6] Furthermore, Bitcoins are not limitless. The creator, Satoshi, set the maximum number of Bitcoins allowed to be in circulation at 21 million.[7] Since its inception in 2009, Bitcoin has over 11 million coins in circulation, more than half of the total available coins.[8]

Acquiring Bitcoins

So how can someone gain possession of Bitcoins? First, an online user must obtain a piece of software, known as a virtual wallet, which allows a user to store and conduct business with the digital currency.[9] Once the digital wallet is acquired, through installation on a computer or mobile device, the user will be able to access the Bitcoin network.[10] The network is the basis for all transactions associated with Bitcoin. While being connected to the Bitcoin network, users can create "coins" by using intense data mining software and hardware tools.[11] Bitcoins are hidden in a complex set of unstructured data.[12] Users are then rewarded with Bitcoins when they are able to solve this complex algorithmic function. These functions increase in difficulty as the amount of coins that are found increase. Many have compared the process to "digging for gold."[13] Due to the difficulty and effort it takes to successfully data mine for coins, users also have an option to take the easy way and purchase Bitcoins from online exchanges. These virtual exchanges, such as mtgox.com and coinbase.com, allow users to purchase and store coins for a currency exchange fee of 1 percent or less.[14]

Bitcoins can be used to purchase goods from retailers and online merchants. However, the list of companies that accepts Bitcoins is relatively small. Companies such as Reddit.com, OKCupid, WordPress, and Foodler accept Bitcoins for its goods and services.[15] Although the list of companies accepting Bitcoins is small, it does not mean that the list will remain small, nor does it mean that companies are not intrigued by the possibilities that digital currency brings.

The Rise of Bitcoin

At the beginning of the year, one Bitcoin was only worth $13.51.[16] However, in April the price for one Bitcoin skyrocketed and traded as high as $270.[17] Now according to online exchanges, such as mxgox.com, one Bitcoin is currently worth approximately $115. Despite its incredibly high volatility, Bitcoin continues to attract investors.

In April, it was reported that Tyler and Cameron Winklevoss owned almost $11 million worth of Bitcoin.[18] You may remember the Winklevoss twins from their legal dispute and settlement with Mark Zuckerberg over the founding of Facebook. The Winklevoss twins are one of the first to publicly announce their backing of Bitcoin. Cameron Winklevoss supported his financial decision, "People really don't want to take it seriously. At some point that narrative will shift to 'virtual currencies are here to stay.' We're in the early days."[19] It is true that Bitcoin is still very much in the early stages. Despite this, Bitcoin has gotten the attention of not only the Winklevoss brothers but also Silicon Valley investment firms that have financed Bitcoin-related companies.[20] Even eBay has announced it will look into new ways of incorporating Bitcoin into its PayPal business operations.[21]

In general, the attraction to virtual currency is mostly due to lower transaction costs from removing financial institution intermediaries. The fees associated with using banks or credit card companies, which are usually passed down to the customer, are eliminated with virtual currency. This is especially helpful when conducting transactions that are low in value, usually less than a few dollars. In addition, another benefit to virtual currencies is the instantaneous exchange and verification of money. Specifically with Bitcoin, without a financial intermediary and with transaction history recording, the exchange of money is seamless and the time it takes to verify is practically immediate. Although virtual currency is not a new concept, Bitcoin has succeeded in areas where its previous predecessors have failed. Bitcoin verifies money is not being double counted or counterfeited using anonymous transaction time stamping.[22] Not only does this ensure immediate exchange and verification but it also allows users to remain anonymous while doing so. Bitcoin has also attracted many users and investors with its approach to control supply.[23] Due to the limited supply, many people speculate that the value of a Bitcoin will continue to increase as the supply decreases. However, as we have seen with past bubbles, speculation will not always lead to financial wealth.

The Associated Risks

There are several legal and ethical implications that arise with any virtual currency, especially when looking at the Bitcoin business model. Bitcoin essentially ensures anonymous transactions over the Internet, which makes it impossible to track the parties involved. This could attract illegal entities such as drug dealers and criminals involved in money laundering. According to many sources, Bitcoin is widely used on Silk Road, an anonymous marketplace that has been linked to the purchase and sale of illegal drugs.[24] Essentially, the anonymous nature of Bitcoin can attract other criminals that have a desire to successfully launder money by exchanging "dirty" money into Bitcoins and then back into "clean" money.

Similar to the conventional currency, digital currency can also be lost or stolen. Since inception, there have been several Bitcoin thefts from hackers.[25] There have also been system crashes that resulted in "lost" currency.[26] Again, lost and stolen currency would be very difficult, nearly impossible, to trace as all users are anonymous. Unlike traditional financial institutions, Bitcoin currency is not backed by insurance of any kind.[27] Once a Bitcoin is lost or stolen, it is gone for good.

Perhaps the biggest risk to Bitcoin is that the concept of virtual currency applied to practice is still in the early stages. It is very possible that consumer confidence in virtual currency becomes so low that it deems Bitcoins valueless.[28] Virtual currency does not have the years of trust nor does it have the regulations that fiat currency has. Years of lawsuits and lobbying have inspired laws and regulations for conventional currencies. If Bitcoin hopes to continue to operate for the long term, a governing body will most likely need to intervene to define what those laws and regulations should be. Financial disclosure is one area in particular that can affect Bitcoin. It was reported earlier this month by The Financial Times that the U.S. Commodity Futures Trading Commission (CFTC) is currently discussing the possibility of Bitcoin being under CFTC jurisdiction, which could make things difficult for virtual currency exchange companies.[29] The managing partner of Union Square Ventures, Fred Wilson, stated his concern for certain regulations on Bitcoin, "If I really sat down and thought about writing a financial disclosure statement, I could probably list dozens of risks."[30]

Conclusion

Many people still believe that virtual currency is speculative and that many signs point to another bubble. The high volatility of Bitcoin was

demonstrated in the large swings that the market
experienced from the beginning of the year until now.
This has proven the market for Bitcoin is still an
unstable one. However, the need for instant, cheaper,
and private transactions will maintain, if not increase,
in the future. Will Bitcoin be the vehicle for these
types of transactions in the future? Time will only tell
where the outlook of virtual currency lies.

---

[1] Needleman, Sarah E. and Ante, Spencer E. "A Bitcoin Primer: What You Need
to Know About the New Virtual Currency." *The Wall Street Journal.* 8
May 2013. Accessed 10 May 2013 <blogs.wsj.com>.

[2] Ibid.

[3] Ibid.

[4] Schutzer, Dan. "Bitcoin and Other Non-Conventional Financial Products."
BITS Financial Services Roundtable. May 2013. Accessed 10 May 2013
<www.bits.org>.

[5] Hathaway, Jay. "Mysterious inventor 'Satoshi Nakamoto' May be Holding $100
million in Bitcoin." *The Daily Dot.* 18 Apr. 2013. Accessed 10 May
2013 <www.dailydot.com>.

[6] Kumar, Nikhil. "The Dazzling Rise And Fall Of The Virtual Currency Bitcoin."
The Independent. 12 Apr. 2013. Accessed 10 May 2013
<www.independent.co.uk>.

[7] Needleman.

[8] Kumar.

[9] Ibid.

[10] Ibid.

[11] Schutzer.

[12] Ibid.

[13] Ibid.

[14] Needleman.

[15] Statt, Nick. "Brave Businesses Buy Into Bitcoin: Is it A Bubble?" *ReadWrite*. 22 Apr 2013. Accessed 10 May 2013 <readwrite.com>.

[16] Sivy.

[17] Kumar.

[18] Popper, Nathaniel and Lattman, Peter. "Never Mind Facebook; Winklevoss Twins Rule in Digital Money." *The New York Times*. 11 Apr 2013. Accessed 10 May 2013 <www.nytimes.com>.

[19] Ibid.

[20] Ibid.

[21] Needleman, Sarah E. and Ante, Spencer E. "Bitcoin Startups Begin to Attract Real Cash." *The Wall Street Journal*. 8 May 2013. Accessed 11 May 2013 <www.wsj.com>.

[22] Sivy, Michael. "The Real Significance of the Bitcoin Boom (and Bust)." *Time Magazine*. 12 Apr 2013. Accessed 11 May 2013 <www.time.com>.

[23] Ibid.

[24] "Mining Digital Gold." *The Economist*. 13 Apr 2013. Accessed 11 May 2013 <www.economist.com>.

[25] Ibid.

[26] Ibid.

[27] Kumar.

[28] Kumar.

[29] Needleman, "Bitcoin Startups."

[30] Ibid.

Mobile Payment Trends

Andrew H. R. Hansen

April 2012

Abstract *– With the constantly changing technological landscape, identifying enduring trends can be difficult. Andrew looks at near-field communication and credit card reading applications, two emerging trends in the mobile payment industry. Each of these products and services utilizes different technologies that allow currency to be transferred. These new technologies introduce new security risks, and Andrew presents recommendations for how consumers and business owners can prepare for these potential changes, and invest the necessary resources into selecting solutions.*

Introduction

There can be no doubt that the rapid technological advances of the previous decade have fundamentally altered the way businesses and consumers interact. But with the constantly changing landscape, it is often difficult to determine which emerging trends will be embraced and incorporated into daily life, and which will be discarded after a brief moment in the spotlight. With the widespread adoption of smartphones, and the more recent proliferation of tablet computers, it should come as no surprise that many developing trends are associated with mobile devices. Trends in

the mobile payments industry have the potential to
impact society in a major way. However, with these
new mobile trends come new risks. As illustrated in a
recent IBM study, "There was a 19 percent increase in
2011 in publicly released exploits aimed at mobile
devices."[1] This research note will provide a general
overview of two mobile payment trends: near field
communication technology and credit card reading
mobile applications, discuss security features and
possible threats and conclude with recommendations
for navigating these emerging technologies.

Mobile Payments

Alternative payment options in the mobile financial
services industry operate under many names,
including: mobile payments, mobile money, mobile
banking, and mobile wallet. Regardless of which term
is preferred, the basic objective behind the mobile
payments movement is to streamline the payment
process by replacing a wallet full of credit cards with a
mobile device. At the influential South by Southwest
Interactive Conference and Festival last month,
mobile payments were a popular topic. Commenting
on the trend, one writer said, "The future of buying
stuff seems like it's going to be cashless, credit card-
less and tied to whatever mobile device you happen to
be carrying around."[2] Although the technology for
mobile payments has existed for some time, 2011 saw

a number of major organizations enter into the industry.[3]

Near Field Communication

Many of these new mobile payment providers share a similar technology called near field communication. Near field communication (NFC) is a "short-range wireless technology that enables the communication between devices over distances of less than 10 cm."[4] As alluded to earlier, this technology is not exactly new or cutting edge. In fact, it is a variation of radio-frequency identification (RFID), a technology utilized in a large variety of products for decades. Similar to RFID, near field communication "can quickly swap information between devices when they're touched together."[5] By producing NFC enabled smartphones, advocates promise there will be no more fussing with a wallet full of credit cards. Instead, "you simply wave your phone at a point-of-sale reader."[6]

NFC technology has been deployed in hundreds of trials, pilots, and tests around the world.[7] Yet consumer adoption has been timid, a characteristic attributed to the fact that the number of establishments that accept mobile payments has been limited.[8] In 2010, "only about 10 percent of total POS (point-of-sale) terminal shipments included some form of contactless technology."[9] However, it is projected that "85 percent of terminals shipped worldwide will be contactless-enabled in 2016, driven by increased proliferation of contactless cards and, especially, rapid adoption of NFC-enabled phones."[10]

The following is a high level description of three prominent organizations that are utilizing NFC technology in their products:

Google Wallet: Google's mobile payment option. Currently only available with the Nexus S 4G on Sprint, and is accepted at over 140,000 MasterCard PayPass locations across the U.S.[11] In time, Google hopes to support all major credit cards.[12] The service is expected to be offered on at least 10 additional phones on Sprint this year.[13]

Isis: A joint venture between Verizon Wireless, AT&T and T-Mobile, expects to launch in limited locations mid-2012.[14] Chase, Capital One, and Barclaycard have all entered agreements to make their debit and credit cards available on Isis.[15]

Apple: Speculated to be a feature of the iPhone 5, with the iWallet, users "can see their entire credit card profiles, view statements and messages form their banks, and even adjust preferences or add additional cards.[16] They can also keep track of their payments and statements within the iTunes billing system.[17]

PayPal: Reportedly partnering with Swedish companies Accumulate and Point, users can download a PayPal in-store iOS or Android app, and when they visit a participating store receive a sticker that allows them to pay via NFC.[18] In addition, they have developed an iPhone app that allows users to transfer money directly from one phone to the other, by bumping the two phones together.[19]

Security

Because NFC mobile payment "reuses the logical and physical security mechanisms used for contactless cards" while offering "additional security layers," it appears that sufficient protection is in place to enable secure transactions.[20] According to security firm Gemalto,[21] the following three key features reinforce Mobile NFC security:

The NFC SIM cards storing a consumer's payment credentials and the payment applications are certified according to security standards defined by financial services authorities and are comparable to CHIP-N-PIN security.

Consumers can choose to authenticate transactions by entering a PIN code on the payment application. Consumers can also request the PIN to be entered for all payments, even for small amounts – providing the end-user with complete control of protection features.

Secure over-the-air technology for remote management enables immediate remote blocking of the payment application.

Even with these additional security layers, one possible risk, specifically associated with Google Wallet, is the lack of encryption for all the data associated with the card.[22] Researchers with Via Forensics report, "While Google Wallet does a decent job securing your full credit card's numbers, the amount of data that Google Wallet stores unencrypted on the device is significant. Many consumers would not find it acceptable if people knew their credit card balance or limits."[23] From the perspective of privacy, it may be valuable to consider how personal consumer information will be monitored and tracked by the NFC enabled devices. Mobile payment services will likely "be used to closely monitor your activity as a consumer… allow(ing) a far closer and more intensive monitoring of this activity."[24] Depending on your tolerance for information security, the unencrypted credit card balance/limits and the use of personal information might not be alarming. Being aware of these risks and making educated mitigation decisions is the critical factor.

Card Readers

The second mobile payment industry trend we will discuss is point-of-sale mobile card readers. This technology combines a simple card reading device and mobile application that allows for the processing of credit card payments. As seen in the images, card readers developed by Square, Intuit and PayPal all offer a similar set of products and services.

25

26

27

After a user signs up for the necessary account with
any of these organizations, they will be mailed a free
card reader. Connecting the card reader through the
earphone plug of an Android- or iOS-powered
smartphone or tablet - then downloading the
necessary mobile app - will transform the mobile

device into a credit card processor. Charges processed by the card reader can be directly transferred into the merchant's bank account, with the service provider collecting a small transaction fee. Some of the benefits described by Intuit[28] include:

- Getting paid instantly
- Process any major credit card
- No need to purchase additional equipment
- Get authorization in seconds – no need to write down payment information or call into your back office
- E-mail or text message clients electronic receipts directly from your phone

In addition, some services like Square's Register, allows merchants to keep track of sales and offer detailed analytics that are synced and stored in the cloud.[29]

Security

Because no credit card information is stored on the phone,[30] these services are secure – or as secure as any other credit card payment method.[31] However, Square has been subject to criticism based upon potential hacking vulnerability. As explained by hackers at a 2011 Black Hat convention, plug-in adapters like those offered by Square (and the other brands previously mentioned), work by converting credit card magstripe data into audio, which is then interpreted by the application and translated back into credit card numbers.[32] With the appropriate software, arbitrary credit card numbers could be fed into the device and fraudulent credit card charges of any amount could be entered.[33] In addition to racking up fraudulent charges, there is also concern that these devices could easily operate as "skimmers." A skimmer is a "device that gathers credit card information during an otherwise legitimate transaction."[34] For example, at a restaurant a server might take a customer credit card out of sight to process their payment, the credit card could be swiped and its information saved, without the customer ever knowing.[35]

An important distinction to make is that the security criticism these products receive is largely aimed at what ill-intentioned people can do with the technology, not necessarily the products and services themselves. Square (and others) claim that because they monitor the entire transaction process, they have the ability to detect and "stop fraud via live monitoring programs that analyze transactions as they're happening."[36] In response to the skimming criticism, Square co-founder Jack Dorsey said to call Square insecure is "not a fair or accurate claim and it overlooks all the protections already built into your credit card."[37] He went on to say, "Any technology – an encrypted card reader, phone camera, or plain old pen and paper – can be used to 'skim' or copy numbers from a credit card… The bank that issues your credit card recognizes this and does not hold you responsible for fraudulent charges."[38] This response might be sufficient for some, but it appears pressure from powerful investment partners like Visa, were finally enough for Square to alter its system to encrypt credit card data on the fly. In very recent news, it appears that Square has started to ship card readers that use encryption.[39] For those using unencrypted plug-in adapters from any brand, moving to the more secure product is worth the effort.

Conclusion

It is expected that NFC technology will become a multi-billion dollar industry[40] whose reach will not only impact mobile payments, but will also affect the travel industry, the way we purchase tickets, comparison shopping, advertising, and possibly several others.[41] Similarly, companies like Square are now processing millions of dollars a day.[42] This research note was intended to be considered from the perspective of both the consumer and the business owner. Whether you are a technologically savvy consumer trying to maximize available technological advances, or a business owner hoping to find new ways to satisfy customer needs, the coming years will likely bring a change to the way money is exchanged.

There are many circumstances where mobile credit card readers like those mentioned previously could easily and instantly affect the business of a small retailer. But from a risk mitigation perspective, there might be some wisdom in allowing the technology and the major players in the NFC mobile payment industry to become more fully established, before investing in their products or services. It is often tempting to respond to major trends by getting on the bandwagon as soon as possible. But manifesting patience and conducting thorough research will ensure the products and services selected will not only be the appropriate solutions, but that they will also be the solutions that endure.

---

[1] "Cyber-Criminals Change Tactics as Network Security Improves." *CIOInsight.* 3 Mar. 2012. Accessed 6 Apr. 2012 <www.cioinsight.com>.

[2] Gallaga, Omar L. "Big Moves in Mobile Payments Could Impact Your Wallet – If You Still Have One." *Statesman.* 1 Apr. 2012. Accessed 4 Apr. 2012. <www.statesman.com>.

[3] "Mobile Payments." *Mashable.* Accessed 4 Apr. 2012 <mashable.com>

[4] "NFC Definition." *Gemalto.com.* n. d. Accessed 4 Apr. 2012 <www.gemalto.com>.

[5] Gardiner, Bryan. "What is Near-Field Communication." *Gizmodo.* 6 Dec. 2010. Accessed 5 Apr. 2012 <gizmodo.com>.

[6] "Mobile Payments and NFC Technology Poised to Revolutionize Retail and Marketing." *NFC Handsets*. n. d. Accessed 4 Apr. 2012 <nfchandsets.com>.

[7] "NFC Trials, Pilots, Tests and Live Services Around the World." *Near Field Communications World*. n. d. Accessed 4 Apr. 2012. <www.nfcworld.com>.

[8] Morales, S. "The Emergence of the Mobile Wallet." *Glyph Interface*. 22 Feb. 2012. Accessed 4 Apr. 2012. <www.cjandp.com>.

[9] Clark, Sarah. "ABI: 85 percent of POS Terminals to Support Contactless Payments in 2012." *Near Field Communications World*. 11 Aug. 2012. Accessed 5 Apr. 2012 <www.nfcworld.com>.

[10] Clark.

[11] "Google Wallet: FAQ." *Google.com*. n. d. Accessed 5 Apr. 2012 <www.google.com>.

[12] "Google Wallet: FAQ."

[13] Melanson, Donald. "Google Wallet Android App Updated, Headed to 'At Least' Ten More Sprint Phones This Year." *Engadget*. 1 Mar. 2012. Accessed 5 Apr. 2012 <www.engadget.com>.

[14] Graziano, Dan. "Google Wallet Competitor ISIS Finally Announces Launch Details." Business Resource Group. 27 Feb. 2012. Accessed 5 Apr. 2012. <www.bgr.com>.

[15] Graziano.

[16] Smith, Dave. "Apple iPhone 5 Release Rumors: 3 New Patents That May Become Features." *International Business Times*. 16 Mar. 2012. Accessed 7 Mar. 2012 <www.ibtimes.com>.

[17] Smith.

[18] Rao, Leena. "PayPal Tests In-Store NFC Payments App With Swedish Retailers, Similar Mobile 'Experiments' to Roll Out Soon." *Techcrunch*. 20 Dec. 2011. Accessed 5 Apr. 2012 <techcrunch.com>.

[19] "Google Checkout vs PayPal vs Amazon Payments: What's the Best eCommerce Option?" *Digital Family*. n. d. Accessed 5 Apr. 2012. <www.digitalfamily.com>

[20] "8 Myths About Mobile NFC – Myth 2." *Gemalto*. n. d. Accessed 5 Apr. 2012 <www.gemalto.com>.

[21] "8 Myths."

[22] Mills, Elinor. "Google Wallet Stores too Much Unencrypted Data in a Rooted
        Device – Report." *CNet News.* 12 Dec. 2011. Accessed 5 Apr. 2012
        <news.cnet.com>.

[23] Mills.

[24] Tristram, Penny. "To Beep or not to Beep – The Pros and Cons of Google
        Wallet." *My Social Agency.* 28 Sept. 2011. Accessed Apr. 5 2012.
        <www.mysocialagency.com>.

[25] Image taken from: www.techclump.com/wp-
        content/uploads/2011/05/full_1293811604Screenshot2010-   12-
        31at10.47.56AM.png

[26] Image taken from: articles.businessinsider.com/2011-02-
        18/tech/29975173_1_android-apps-readers-comparison-chart

[27] Image taken from: smallbiztrends.com/2012/03/paypal-here.html

[28] "Intuit GoPayment Mobile Credit Card Processing." *Intuit.* n. d. Accessed 5
        Apr. 2012 <payments.intuit.com>.

[29] "Square Register for iPad Offers Full Point-of-Sale System for Merchants." 5
        Mar. 2012. Accessed 5 Apr. 2012 <www.appleinsider.com>.

[30] "Intuit GoPayment."

[31] Gobry, Pascal-Emmanuel. "Verifone is Full of Crap – Square is Totally
        Secure." *Business Insider.* 10 Mar. 2011. Accessed 5 Apr. 2012
        <articles.businessinsider.com>

[32] Schwartz, Matthew J. "iPad Credit Card Reader Hacked as Skimmer."
        InformationWeek Security. 5 Aug. 2011. Accessed 5 Apr. 2012
        <www.informationweek.com>.

[33] Schwartz.

[34] Hornshaw, Phil. "Researchers Reveal Two Security Gaps in Square Mobile
        Credit Card Reader." *Appolicious.* 8 Aug. 2011. Accessed 5 Apr. 2012
        <www.appolicious.com>.

[35] Hornshaw.

[36] "Security is our Priority." *Square.com.* n. d. Accessed 5 Apr. 2012
        <www.squareup.com>

[37] Crum, Chris. "Square Security Defended by CEO Jack Dorsey." *WebProNews.*
        10 Mar. 2011. Accessed 5 Apr. 2012 <www.webpronews.com>.

[38] Crum.

[39] Crum, Chris. "Square Card Readers Now Reportedly Encrypted."
        WebProNews.27 Mar. 2012. Accessed 7 Apr. 2012
        <www.webpronews.com>.

[40] Smith.

[41] Robertson, Travis. "Eight Industries That Will Benefit From NFC
        Technology." *X.Commerce*. 19 Apr. 2011. Accessed 5 Apr. 2012
        <www.x.com>.

[42] Schonfeld, Erick. "Processing $11 Million a Day, Jack Dorsey Says: "We don't
        Want to Make Square all About Taxi Cabs." *Techcrunch*. 13 Nov.
        2011. Accessed 5 Apr. 2012 <techcrunch.com>.

The Mobile Banking Phenomenon

Devin Luco

April 2012

Abstract – *Accessing a bank account statement, making account transfers, and even cashing checks via a picture are all functions that financial institutions are increasingly supporting via mobile websites and apps designed for smartphones and tablets. Devin discusses these rising trends in mobile banking, the risks that mobile users should be aware of, and how to securely use mobile banking.*

Introduction

In terms of speed, storage, and bandwidth, mobile smartphones are exponentially more powerful than our earliest personal computers. This should not be surprising due to theories, such as Moore's Law, that have predicted trends of this nature to continue as our technology advances. Maybe the most astounding part of smartphones is not in its power, but in its size. The devices that we now use for everyday computing tasks, tasks that once required a personal desktop computer, are handheld and mobile. Our daily casual Internet browsing, information searches, social media interactions, gaming, shopping, and banking can be conveniently completed through our smartphones while on the go. In fact, mobile Internet usage is projected to exceed Internet usage from desktop computers by 2014.[1] Companies are beginning to understand this trend and adjust business models accordingly to cater to the needs of the changing consumer.

Mobile Banking

Financial institutions, which historically have conducted face-to-face transactions for retail banking, are becoming flexible and finding new ways to appeal to the mobile consumer. Deposits, transfers, payments, and account information requests can all be fulfilled through mobile applications available in an application store, such as Apple's App Store or Android's Marketplace. In addition, less complicated tasks such as requesting a balance or finding a local ATM can be completed through Text and SMS Banking. There are also third-party applications that may be linked to an individual's bank account for payment services. Third-party applications, such as Venmo, are used for mobile payment services to friends and families.[2] Although the concept of mobile banking is recent, there are more users now than a year ago. According to a March 2013 Federal Reserve report, 48 percent of smartphone users, as of November 2012, said they have used mobile banking within the past 12 months.[3] This is an increase from the 42 percent in December 2011.[4] According to the report, 87 percent checked an account balance or transaction, 53 percent transferred funds and 21 percent deposited a check.[5] While the usage of mobile banking is increasing, it is important to note that there are a large number of users still not using phones for banking. Despite the convenience, mobile banking also brings inherent risks.

Risks of Mobile Banking

It is hard to deny the benefits of mobile banking. The fact that mobile banking still has lots of room to grow, in terms of customer base, brings the question: Why are there so many people still not using mobile banking? Could the risks outweigh the benefits? Is mobile banking truly riskier than traditional online banking? Certainly there are end-user risks that are not necessarily there with personal computers. According to a study by Morgan Stanley, 91 percent of those surveyed said that they have their cell phones within an arm's reach 24 hours a day.[6] Smartphones are carried with individuals at all times, which means the chances that the device is lost or stolen is much greater than losing a computer. Whenever a personal device falls into the wrong hands, privacy of the victim is in jeopardy. Unless the data on the phone is encrypted or password protected, the information can be retrieved with relative ease. Nevertheless, most banks usually do not store login credentials in browsers or mobile applications without the users' permission. Unless the user stored credentials on the device, the unauthorized person will most likely not be able to access any banking information. However, if a phone is lost or stolen, the unauthorized person will have access to everything on the phone, including text messages, contacts, and other non-protected applications. This means that if your banking protection (login, password, etc.) is weak then sophisticated hackers may be able to find a way to break into your accounts. This can be alleviated with additional authentications (locked phones, passwords to use applications) and stronger passwords.

Other threats to mobile banking include remote hackers and malware attacks. The danger of malware attacks stems from lack of awareness. Mobile devices are similar to computers in the sense that they also can be infected with viruses or malicious code. Usually this is from users not being as careful as they would be on a personal computer. Users should exercise caution when accessing their banking information through smartphones. Trusted anti-virus and spyware software should also be installed on mobile devices to protect against malware. Malware can also infect a mobile device through third-party applications. Often users download applications that they may think are safe, such as games or utilities, but end up with malware. In 2011, Google removed several malicious applications that Symantec estimated to have been downloaded between 50,000 and 200,000 times.[7] The type of infection that can result from mobile malware includes: activity monitoring, data retrieval, system modification, and unauthorized connectivity.[8] If a user is sending sensitive text messages, storing sensitive information or accessing mobile banking through an infected smartphone, the hacker can gain all of this information for mischievous purposes. It is important to conduct extensive research of third-party applications before downloading them onto your device. Cross check reviews and look online to make sure the application is safe to download. Mobile banking applications from financial institutions are usually safe. Applications offered by financial institutions create a direct connection between the user and the bank without the need of a middle-man (third-party application or browser).[9] This gives financial institutions more control over the security and can offer a number of options that will add to the user's privacy. Financial institutions can implement further protections such as secure sockets layer (SSL) encryption, multiple authentications and remote data wiping.[10] However, when a malicious application is downloaded it can greatly affect a customer's mobile banking experience as credentials can be stolen regardless of how secure the financial institution's application may be.

Conclusion

As more users continue to use mobile devices for everyday tasks, including mobile banking, the security threats will become more advanced and prevalent on mobile devices. Traditional online banking has been around for years, which has spawned stronger security measures to mitigate the vast amounts of Internet threats. While mobile banking is still in its infancy stages, protection against unauthorized users and malware attacks is still dependent on the users. Protection can be achieved through awareness and caution when downloading third-party applications. It is never a good idea to store sensitive information onto your mobile device or browsers. Additional precautions should be taken in the event the mobile device is lost or stolen. Furthermore, remote data wipes can control the damage if an unauthorized person gains access to the device. In any case, the risks of mobile banking can be mitigated if the user is cautious and aware.

---

[1] Richmond, Holly. "The Growth of Mobile Marketing and Tagging." Microsoft Tag. 21 Mar 2011. Accessed 8 Jun 2013 <tag.microsoft.com>.

[2] Wortham, Jenna. "After 2 Years of Testing, Venmo Opens Payment Service to Public." *The New York Times*. 20 Mar 2012. Accessed 8 Jun 2013 <nytimes.com>.

[3] Geffner, Marcie. "More People Using Mobile Banking." Bankrate. 5 Apr 2013.
Accessed 8 Jun 2013 <www.bankrate.com>.

[4] Geffner.

[5] Geffner.

[6] Daffern, Pete. "Mobile Banking Is More Secure Than Online Banking."
BusinessWeek. Feb 2012. Accessed 8 Jun 2013
<www.businessweek.com>.

[7] Claburn, Thomas. "Google Removes Malicious Android Apps."
InformationWeek Security. 2 Mar 2011. Accessed 9 Nov 2012
<www.informationweek.com>.

[8] Glynn, Fergal. "Mobile Security: Prevent Mobile Application Code Security
Risks." Veracode. Accessed 8 Jun 2013 <www.veracode.com>.

[9] Matthews, Tim. "Don't Be Afraid of Mobile Banking Apps." *Bank Systems and
Technology*. 5 Sept 2012. Accessed 8 Jun 2013 <www.banktech.com>.

[10] Matthews.

Whistleblowers and the Dodd-Frank Act

Devin Luco

October 2012

Abstract – *Protecting the rights of whistleblowers – people informing on others who are engaged in illegal/unethical behavior - has been a major topic of public conversation, particularly since the 2008 financial crisis. Everyone seems to agree accountability is important, though not everyone can agree on what the checks and balances should look like. Devin examines why whistleblowing is important, the difference between internal and external whistleblowers, and how the 2010 Dodd-Frank Act impacts whistleblower programs.*

Introduction

In recent years, we have seen large companies such as Enron, WorldCom, and Lehman Brothers fall due to ethical and financial misconduct. In the case of Enron and WorldCom, profits and assets were heavily inflated by using creative but fraudulent accounting strategies. On the other hand, unethical lending standards were implemented at Lehman Brothers in order to make housing affordable during the rise of the U.S. housing bubble. All three of these situations not only caused their firms to declare bankruptcy but also cost millions of dollars for employees, investors, and the Federal Government.

One might ask how fraudulent activities were not caught before so much damage struck? In many cases, employees were aware of these activities well in advance of financial failure. However, these companies did not have a culture where confronting unethical practices was encouraged. In one example, Cynthia Cooper, internal auditor for WorldCom, brought forward an internal audit to the Board of Directors Auditing Committee even though the CFO asked that she delay her investigation. However, by that time it was too late and failure was imminent.[1]

So, what protections or processes are in place for individuals that want to bring these illegal or corrupt activities forward? This act is commonly known as "whistleblowing" and just recently has the Securities and Exchange Commission implemented such protections to encourage people to bring corporate corruption to justice.

Whistleblowers

In the 1970s Ralph Nader was one of the first people to devise the term "whistleblower" or "whistleblowing." According to him, "Whistleblowing is an act of a man or woman who, believing that the public interest overrides the interest of the organization he serves, blows the whistle that the organization is in corrupt, illegal, fraudulent or harmful activity."[2] Although this overarching definition is true, there are two types of whistleblowers: internal and external. Internal whistleblowers refer to those that find unethical behavior or illegal misconduct within their organization and reports it up the chain-of-command. In contrast, external whistleblowers will report to an outside organization such as the Securities and Exchange Commission (SEC).[3]

Internal whistleblower programs are the last line of defense before employees report to an outside party and eventually cause millions of dollars in financial consequence. However, it is understandable why employees historically have hesitated to speak up. Companies were able to fire employees at any given moment before the 1960s. In the late 1970s, federal and state legislations were passed such as anti-discrimination legislations, Truth in Lending laws, the Fair Credit Reporting Act, and the Environmental Protection Act, which were intended to protect the community from illegal practices. Over the years, many laws have been created for governmental purposes but not so many for the private sector.[4] To put this into context, in the early 2000s new laws were just passed to give stronger protections for individuals working in public firms. According to Steven Kohn, whistleblower protections were implemented through the Sarbanes-Oxley Act Section 806, 18 U.S.C. 1514A, which was spurred by the classic accounting cases of Enron and WorldCom in 2002.[5] Nevertheless, federal legislation that was recently passed in 2010 has reshaped the earlier whistleblower program by providing protections and incentives for employees in publically traded firms: The Dodd-Frank Act.

Dodd-Frank Act and Impacts

The Dodd-Frank Act was enacted in 2010, which allowed whistleblowers to report information to the SEC that could lead to possible sanctions over $1 million.[6] Individuals would collect a range of 10 percent to 30 percent of the money that is collected by the SEC.[7] On top of that, employees are protected under this law from employer retaliation.[8] According to Section 922 of the Dodd-Frank Act, the following protections are administered:[9]

Prohibition of Retaliation – no employer can discharge or discriminate based on the lawful act of the whistleblower. If discharge or discrimination takes place, the whistleblower is protected under this act and may bring the case forward in the U.S. District Court. In addition, the whistleblower is entitled to relief from the employer that includes reinstatement with same seniority status, two months back pay, and coverage of litigation costs.

Confidentiality – the SEC Commission will not disclose any information provided by the whistleblower, which could reveal the identity of the individual.

Rights retained – all federal and state rights will be retained.

The first payout issued under the program was awarded in August 2012 to an individual who helped the SEC interrupt a multi-million dollar fraud deal. The award was 30 percent, the maximum allowed under Dodd-Frank, of the $150,000 that was collected at the time. Although, during the Obama Administration the SEC has paid out upwards of $1.6 billion dollars,[10] one must look at the amount of money the government has collected. Since 2009, the government has collected $13.2 billion dollars through the False Claims Act alone, which is the "bread and butter" of the whistleblower program.[11] According to SEC Enforcement Director Robert Khuzami, "Had this whistleblower not helped to uncover the full dimensions of the scheme, it is very likely that many more investors would have been victimized."[12] As Mr. Khuzami alluded to, these payouts are a small fraction compared to the money that is being collected from deterring fraudulent activities. Furthermore, the impacts to the financial markets would be devastating as well.

Proponents of the newly refined whistleblower program have argued that the program has "turned anti-fraud efforts into a lottery."[13] They are afraid that employees will turn to the SEC instead of reporting misconduct internally first in search of a big payout. In one instance, a whistleblower has already received $104 million.[14] However, studies conducted by the Ethics Research Center have shown that 2 percent of whistleblowers went directly to an external party without reporting internally first.[15] The studies further showed that 82 percent would report big fraudulent crimes to an outside party but only 43 percent would do it solely for the reward.[16] This study shows that employees still respect internal whistleblowing programs and would only seek external help if the misconduct is severe and employers have not responded to the situation in a timely matter.

Conclusion

While we have seen many reforms in the past, whether it is to regulate the government or private sector, the Dodd-Frank Act is one that has displayed traction. We have witnessed the SEC pay out its' first award in August 2012, only two years after the program was created. If we look at the awards as well as the amount of tips that are being sent to the SEC (about eight tips a day),[17] one can conclude that employees are feeling more comfortable than ever reporting illegal behavior. However, the government's involvements in these cases are not always needed if the company has an established internal whistleblower program. Evidence has shown that employees are willing to look internally before seeking the protection offered by the Dodd-Frank Act.

---

[1] Ravishankar, by Lilanthi. "Encouraging Internal Whistleblowing in Organizations." Santa Clara University - Markkula Center for Applied Ethics 1 Jan. 2003. Accessed 4 Oct. 7, 2012 <www.scu.edu>.

[2] Rongine, Nicholas M. "Toward a Coheren Legal Response to the Public Policy Dilemma Posed by Whistleblowing." *American Business Law Journal.* 1985.

[3] Kietzman, Shannon. "What Is a Whistleblower?" *wiseGeek.* 23 Jul. 2012. Accessed 4 Oct. 2012 <www.wisegeek.com>.

[4] Ravishankar.

[5] Kohn, Stephen M. "Sarbanes-Oxley Act: Legal Protection for Corporate Whistleblowers." NWC - National Whistleblowers Center. n.d. Accessed 4 Oct. 2012 <www.whistleblowers.org>.

[6] "SEC Issues First Whistleblower Program Award." U.S. Securities and Exchange Commission. 21 Aug. 2012. Accessed 4 Oct. 2012 <www.sec.gov>.

[7] SEC.

[8] SEC.

[9] "Dodd-Frank Act Subtitle B-Increasing Regulatory Enforcement and Remedies." U.S. Securities and Exchange Commission. 21 Jul. 2010. Accessed 4 Oct. 2012 <www.sec.gov>.

[10] Lipton, Eric. "A Legal Circle Reaches Deep to Aid Obama." *The New York Times.* 1 Oct. 2012. Accessed 4 Oct. 2012 <www.nytimes.com>.

[11] Lipton.

[12] Gallu, Joshua. "SEC Pays $50,000 in First Dodd-Frank Whistleblower Reward." *Bloomberg.* 21 Aug. 2012. Accessed 4 Oct. 2012 <www.bloomberg.com>.

[13] Lipton.

[14] Lipton.

[15] Matthews, C.M. "Most Whistleblowers Report Internally, Study Finds." *Wall Street Journal.* 30 May 2012. 4 Oct. 2012 Accessed <www.blog.wsj.com>.

[16] Matthews.

[17] SEC.

Chapter IV
Data Security

Engaging in Cyber Warfare

Devin Luco
March 2013

Abstract – *Cyber warfare – the battles that rage in digital space are inherently exponentially larger that their physically-bound counterparts. The fallout and effects from cyber warfare are capable of crossing borders and continents in the blink of an eye, affecting government operations and citizens alike. Devin looks in particular at how cyber warfare is playing out between countries, including the U.S. and China, and highlights the critical need to establish rules for governing cyber warfare.*

Introduction

Most people are aware of the most common physical domains in which global warfare takes place: land, water, aerial, and space. More specifically and recently, the world has witnessed international fears regarding nuclear testing and the development of weapons of mass destruction (WMD). North Korea has recently threatened to conduct nuclear testing despite opposition from the United Nations (UN). The North Korean government also has increased hostility against the U.S. and on many occasions resisted negotiating terms in regards to nuclear testing. The possibility that North Korea will potentially possess the capability to develop WMD has created great danger for the U.S. and other members of the United Nations. As these tensions will continue to be watched closely over the course of the year and future years, the U.S. is facing another form of warfare: cyber warfare.

What is Cyber Warfare?

Cyber warfare describes a politically influenced type of warfare conducted by a certain country or hostile organization (such as a terrorist group) that aims at spying on or sabotaging another country.[1] According to security specialists, there are numerous types of cyber warfare, which include "sabotage, electrical power grid, vandalism, and information gathering."[2] In an October 2012 speech, former U.S. Secretary of Defense Leon Panetta stated the dangers of cyber warfare included the fact that "an aggressor nation or extremist group could use these kinds of cyber-tools to gain control of critical switches."[3] He explained further, saying that:

"They could derail passenger trains or, even more dangerous, derail passenger trains loaded with lethal chemicals. They could contaminate the water supply in major cities or shut down the power grid across large parts of the country."[4]

The reality is that a cyber-war could cripple the U.S., particularly since it could take weeks or even months to repair the damage done by malicious code or hacking. If a hostile nation or organization decided to shut down or take over systems that control U.S. critical infrastructures, such as electricity, oil, water, gas, and transportation, the country would be in chaos. Daily living depends on the consistent functionality of critical infrastructures to the point where many may even take them for granted. As Panetta stated, the disruption in such processes could result in the inability to pump gas, failure to control ground and air traffic, and result in deadly contaminants leaking into water systems.

New Game, New Rules

While the struggle to understand what cyber warfare entails and the effect it may have on a nation continues, it is clear that no existing global rules currently govern this type of warfare. In terms of nuclear warfare, there is a general international understanding that the development of WMD should not be pursued and certainly should not be used on against any nation. Nations such as North Korea, which oppose this general understanding, are in the minority. Ramin Mehmanparast, the Foreign Ministry spokesman of Iran, was quoted saying "We think we need to come to a point where no country will have any nuclear weapons."[5] He went on to say, "all weapons of mass destruction and nuclear arms need to be destroyed."[6] Mehmanparast's statement clearly exemplifies a global understanding that the development of nuclear weapons will not be tolerated. However, this type of understanding and agreement has not been yet established for cyber warfare.

The need for international rules exists due to the severe damage that can be caused by cyber-attacks. Similar to nuclear warfare, where mutually assured destruction is guaranteed if initiated, cyber warfare will not have any winners or losers – just losers. While global rules restrict the use of nuclear weapons against other nations in order to preserve the lives civilians and prisoners of war, in cyber warfare hostile nations can essentially cut another nation's water supply, electrical grid, and military defenses through mainframe and network hacking.[7] Damages are not limited there, as information gathered through cyber-attacks can include the overall elimination of privacy and intellectual property theft.[8]

The UN may be best suited for the job to define rules to cyber war. However, this task is easier said than done. Issues can arise when defining what qualifies as a cyber-warfare attack, or the more difficult task of determining from where cyber-attacks originate.[9] Fears will continue to increase without rules being defined or national standards established on how to approach defending against cyber-attacks. President Barack Obama recently signed an executive order to help protect the U.S. critical infrastructures from cyber-attacks.[10] In this executive order, government officials are directed to work with companies that support critical infrastructures to establish standards around decreasing cyber security threats and vulnerabilities.[11] The order also incentivizes companies to accept and implement these security standards within their own organizations.[12] However, the order does not require companies to share information with each other.[13] In regards to cyber security, information sharing among companies would most definitely help create stronger standards and best practices when defending against cyber-attacks. However, those that oppose information sharing express concerns regarding corporate privacy and competitive advantage.

President Obama's executive order is a great first step to protecting nations and establishing a universal standard that can be implemented globally. According to Mandiant, a U.S. digital-security company, China has been the source of over 100 cyber-attacks on the U.S. (including both public and private entities).[14] The same report claims that a building outside of Shanghai is responsible for these

numerous cyber-attacks.[15] Mandiant states that the
group of hackers housed in this building is known as
Unit 61398.[16] The U.S. accuses Unit 61398 to be under
the authority of the People's Liberation Army but
representatives from Beijing have denied all
allegations.[17] Regardless, the report is shocking, as
they have traced attacks on 141 companies within 20
different industries to this unit.[18] Although the attacks
have been to many different countries, the U.S. has
been the receiving end on a majority of these attacks.
Since 2006, the Chinese hacker unit has committed
141 cyber-attacks but 115 of those attacks were
directed towards U.S. companies.[19] As cyber-attacks
continue to increase, creating a universal
understanding will be more important than ever.

Conclusion

Similar to treaties and agreements in place among
many of the world powers regarding various types of
warfare, nations will need to come to an agreement
on how cyber warfare should be handled. However, to
accomplish this nations will need to first define what
constitutes cyber warfare. Additionally, nations will
need to establish standards on how to protect against
cyber-attacks and how to best identify cyber threats.
The executive order set forth by President Obama will
help establish international norms on how to protect
against cyber-attacks. However, this is only the

beginning of the process. A sizable leap forward will need to take place in order to institute international norms regarding cyber warfare in general. Nations will continue to watch the U.S. and China closely, as cyber war tensions continue to rise.

---

[1] "What is Cyberwarfare?" *SecPoint.com*. Accessed 5 Mar. 2013. < www.secpoint.com>

[2] "What is Cyberwarfare?"

[3] Daly, Michael. "U.S. Not Ready for Cyber War Hostile Hackers Could Launch." *The Daily Beast*. 21 Feb. 2013. Accessed 5 Mar. 2013. <www.thedailybeast.com>.

[4] Daly.

[5] Cowell, Alan. "Iran Is Said to Convert Enriched Uranium to Fuel." *New York Times*. Accessed 12 Feb. 2013. Accessed 5 Mar 2013 <www.nytimes.com>.

[6] Cowell.

[7] Monitor's Editorial Board. "Wanted: Global Rules on Cyberwarfare." *The Christian Science Monitor*. 19 Feb. 2013. Accessed 6 Mar. 2013 <www.csmonitor.com>.

[8] Monitor's Editorial Board.

[9] Monitor's Editorial Board.

[10] Selyukh, Alina. "Obama Executive Order Seeks Better Defense Against Cyber Attacks." *Yahoo News*. 12 Feb. 2013. Accessed 8 Mar. 2013 <www.news.yahoo.com>.

[11] Selyukh.

[12] Selyukh.

[13] Selyukh.

[14] Monitor's Editorial Board.

[15] "U.S. and China Accuse Each Other of Cyberwarfare." *Reuters*. 20 Feb. 2013. Accessed 8 Mar. 2013 <www.rt.com>.

[16] Reuters.

[17] Reuters.

[18] Reuters.

[19] "U.S. Losing Global Cyber War to China – House Intelligence Chairman."
       Reuters. 25 Feb. 2013. Accessed 9 Mar. 2013 <www.rt.com>.

Malware Analysis: A Look Into the Past and Future

Devin Luco
November 2012

Abstract – *This research note defines malware and distinguishes between the different types that users are exposed to today. Devin explains why it is important to keep up-to-date on malware issues, and how it affects millions of users and costs billions of dollars every year. By looking at the 2007 Storm Worm case, Devin paints a clearer picture of why it is important to be cautious when using computers or mobile devices. Most importantly, this note ends with basic steps on how to protect against malware threats in the future.*

What is Malware?

Malware, also known as malicious software, is any code or program that is used to gain access to, collect personal information from, or interrupt the functionality of a private computer. Usually people make the mistake of grouping all malware as "computer viruses." However, there are many different types of malware including Trojan horses, worms, viruses, spyware, and adware.

Trojan Horses – Just as the name implies, Trojan horses conceal themselves as a harmless program but when executed, unleashes a malicious code that damages the operating system of a computer.[1] Often, Trojans are sent via email using misrepresenting messages to manipulate the recipient into opening the program.[2]

Worms – This malicious code has the ability to replicate and distribute itself through networks. Depending on the type of worm, it can replicate with or without user execution. Due to its replicating nature, worms use a vast amount of system resources sometimes resulting in a denial-of-service (making a network service unavailable to its' intended users).[3]

Viruses – Unlike worms, viruses replicate themselves by latching onto a host program or file and spread once the user executes the host.[4] Viruses damage software, hardware, and computer data.

Spyware – Spyware is best known as tracking software. Usually users download this without knowing because it is packaged within another program that the user actually wants.[5] Once installed, Spyware tracks and gathers sensitive information without the user's knowledge. The owner of the spyware can sell the personal information or use it for his/her own malicious purposes.

Adware – Adware is software that displays advertisements to the user.[6] This type of software is usually more of an annoyance for those that are affected. However, some Adware invades a user's privacy with an added tracking function.

Why is it Important?

So why should we care? Malware has been around for many years. Despite anti-virus software protections, malware still infects countless computers across the globe every year. According to a 2010 survey by Symantec, 286 million different types of malware accounted for 3 billion attacks on users.[7] The study also showed high vulnerability for threats on social networking sites, where information on profiles are used for attacks.[8] Attackers target social networking users by linking to malicious sites where they are exposed and exploited.[9] This vulnerability is alarming considering Facebook, one of the most popular social networking sites in the world, just reached one billion users in October 2012. Meaning approximately one-seventh of the world's population could potentially be vulnerable to attacks.

As technology continues to advance, attackers become more sophisticated and find new ways to cause threats. Currently in our society, we are seeing a migration of users from computers to mobile devices. According to a 2012 survey by Pew Research Center,

44 percent of U.S. adults own a smartphone, and 18 percent own a tablet.[10] With the increasing number of mobile users, security threats become more accessible and prevalent. Mobile users usually download many applications from Apple's App Store or Android's Marketplace, which is where malware could possibly be hiding. Google announced in the past that they had to remove several malicious applications, most of them Trojans.[11]

Whether the malware attacks are through computers or mobile devices, it is very costly for consumers. 71 million consumers in the U.S. alone lost $20.7 billion to cybercriminals.[12] Consumers worldwide lost $110 billion from malware attacks during the same period from July 2011 to July 2012.[13]

Storm Worm, considered one of the top 10 worst computer viruses of all time,[14] affected millions of users around the world. By looking at this historical example, we can further our understanding of how malware affects computers and networks, why it spreads so quickly, and how to protect ourselves from future threats.

A Historical Case: The "Storm Worm" Trojan

Storm Worm is a family of Trojan viruses that started infecting Windows based computers in late January 2007.[15] Similar to malware in the past, Storm Worm was sent to computers via email messages with an accompanying attachment. The email would contain a subject line about a natural disaster that occurred. An example of a Storm Worm email subject line would be, "230 dead as storm batters Europe."[16]

The main trap of Storm Worm is the fact the subject line seems real. By using a subject line that describes a natural disaster, recipients are prone to open the email and attachment. The body of the email usually directs the recipient to open the attachment to learn more about the story.[17] Social engineering, a manipulation tactic that takes advantage of human's trusting nature, is the main strategy in this attack. Recipients are trusting the email is legitimate based on the emotional aspect and real nature of the story. Once the file is opened, the infected computer becomes part of a botnet.[18] A botnet describes a group of computers that have been compromised. The hacker can later use and communicate with other compromised computers for malicious purposes without the original owner's knowledge.[19] The Storm Worms botnet was much harder to track and destroy because it did not use a centralized server. Instead, each infected computer acted as a host and was only a section of the entire botnet network.[20]

The Storm Worm is much more complex than other malware. It has several different components:

- A backdoor that allows hackers access for gathering personal information[21]
- The ability to turn computers into spam-bots to generate and post spam to others[22]
- The installation of a peer-to-peer network that allows communication between other infected computers in the botnet[23]
- The ability to gather email address information to spread the virus virtually[24]
- The ability to update and invite other malware programs to download[25]
- A rootkit, which disguises the Trojan[26]

How to Protect Yourself?

Although computing users are exposed to millions of threats every day, there are some easy steps for protecting against malicious software:

For both business and personal users:

Being educated in the different types and the possible damage that can be caused is the first step to protecting yourself from such threats. Reading websites, such as http://www.securityfocus.com/, regularly will help keep you current on malware and vulnerability trends.

Do not open any suspicious emails. Remember, malware can access email address books to distribute itself through email. Advise your colleagues, friends, and families to be cautious with opening attachments as well.

For business users:

Encourage the development of a risk management process. Having a strong risk management methodology will help employees identify controls that are vulnerable to threats, develop plans for mitigating exposure, and develop recovery plans if affected by malware.

Restrict employees' access to buildings, networks, servers, and workstations. Implement access privileges that require employees to enter user ids and passwords.

For personal users:

Update your operating system, browser, and anti-virus software. This will ensure that your machine is prepared to identify the latest malware threats that are circling through the network.

Install malware removal software. This will come in handy if a worm or Trojan bypasses your anti-virus software.

For mobile protection, remember to investigate and research applications before you download. Be sure to

take notice of the developer name and pricing
information - compare it to what you are seeing in the
apps store for any discrepancies.[27]

Conclusion

As we have seen, malware can disguise itself in many
shapes and forms. Malware can be a minor nuisance
as adware or spyware. It can also be very damaging
and costly as Trojans, worms, or viruses. Although we
can never be 100 percent safe, by analyzing and
learning from past malware occurrences, we can be
proactive in preventing and responding to future
attacks.

---

[1] "Strategies for Managing Malware Risks." Microsoft. 18 Aug. 2006. Accessed 6
        Nov. 2012 <technet.microsoft.com>.

[2] Microsoft.

[3] Microsoft.

[4] Microsoft.

[5] Microsoft.

[6] Microsoft.

[7] Oran, Olivia. "Symantec Reports Rise of Malware in Mobile." *The Street*. 4 May
        2010. Accessed 7 Nov. 2012 <www.thestreet.com>.

[8] Oran.

[9] Oran.

[10] Mitchell, Amy, Tom Rosenstiel, and Leah Christian. "Mobile Devices and
        News Consumption: Some Good Signs for Journalism." State of the
        Media. n.d. Accessed 8 Nov. 2012 <www.stateofthemedia.org>.

[11] Claburn, Thomas. "Google Removes Malicious Android Apps."
        InformationWeek Security. 2 Mar. 2011. Accessed 9 Nov. 2012
        <www.informationweek.com>.

[12] Osborne, Charlie. "Cybercrime Costs U.S. Consumers \$20.7 billion." CNET. 5
    Sept. 2012. Accessed 8 Nov. 2012 <www.news.cnet.com>

[13] Osborne.

[14] Strickland, Jonathan. "10 Worst Computer Viruses of All Time."
    HowStuffWorks. n.d. Accessed 6 Nov 2012
    <www.computer.howstuffworks.com>

[15] Kawamoto, Dawn. "'Storm Worm' Rages Across the Globe." CNET. 19 Jan.
    2007. Accessed 30 Oct. 2012 <news.cnet.com>.

[16] Kawamoto.

[17] Kawamoto.

[18] Landesman, Mary. "What is the Storm Worm?" About.com, n.d. Accessed 30
    Oct .2012. <www.antivirus.about.com>.

[19] Landesman.

[20] Landesman.

[21] Landesman.

[22] Landesman.

[23] Landesman.

[24] Landesman.

[25] Landesman.

[26] Landesman.

[27] Jeffers, David. "Protect Your Smartphone from Mobile Malware." *PC World*.
    27 Mar. 2012. Accessed 8 Nov. 2012 <www.pcworld.com>.

Building Resiliency in the IT Sector

Rashmi Shekhar

May 2013

Abstract: In this research note, Rashmi identifies some of the key cyber risks that pose a threat to the functioning of Information Technology in the public and private sectors. Based on a review of the current preventive and remedial measures in place, Rashmi identifies recommendations for building greater resiliency.

Introduction

Information Technology (IT) poses a potent risk to U.S. critical infrastructure, because IT is increasingly pervasive in modern society. Every industry depends on IT to manage core business processes. As a result, the risks involved in the implementation of IT have potential ramifications across other critical infrastructure sectors such as healthcare, energy, chemicals, manufacturing, communication and ultimately the nation's economy.

IT Risks and the Federal Government

In the government sector, the primary IT risks are largely security related. The information systems used by the various U.S. departments all collect, store, process and transmit sensitive information. Consider the Department of Homeland Security (DHS). A mandate of the DHS is to protect the nation from cyber-related crimes. The DHS issues a number of mandates; frameworks and assessments to help organizations and individuals protect, recover from, and report cybercrimes and intrusions that could be potentially harmful to the privacy of citizens or the safety of the country. Therefore, the DHS must deal with a vast amount of security-related information, making data and systems vulnerable to IT-related operational risks.

The systems used by the employees who work in the DHS and the data stores and servers face intrusion risks. There are a number of insurgents who would benefit from this kind of information. The Factor Analysis of Information Risk (FAIR) framework describes the different ways in which threat agents may use information assets – "access, misuse, disclose, modify and deny access to legitimate users."[1],[2] Considering the nature of data handled by the various federal government agencies, any of these actions could lead to dire consequences.

Information systems can be made secure only to a certain extent. Beyond this, the aspect of human limitation comes into picture. From a risk perspective, people are often the weakest link in most organizations. Personnel who work in these offices, especially those with authorized access to sensitive information, pose a threat of information leakage, intentional or otherwise.

IT operational risks also include physical security, since physical damage to the storage devices and systems can be as crippling as the loss due to software crashes or cyber intrusions. Factors affecting physical damage are further discussed in the section below.

In addition to the physical security threats, another important concern related to IT risks is the widespread use in the operation of critical sectors such as the power grid, healthcare systems, and nuclear power stations.[3] Industrial control systems such as SCADA (Supervisory Control and Data Acquisition) are responsible for controlling and monitoring critical infrastructure components such as power and nuclear generators, water purification plants, waste management plants, chemical treatment plants and the like. Thus, the other critical infrastructure sectors identified by the DHS depend upon the working of IT. In these sensitive and mission critical contexts, there is no room for system- and process-based errors.

Current Risk Mitigation Policies and Systems
A number of federal agencies and regulations have been put in place to help mitigate IT risks to the

critical infrastructure of the nation. The Department of Homeland Security's National Cyber Security Division (NCSD) was constituted in order to develop and implement an effective risk management and response program.[4]

Government networks are currently protected by intrusion detection software called EINSTEIN developed by the U.S. Computer Emergency Readiness Team (U.S.-CERT) of the NCSD.[5],[6],[7] EINSTEIN acts like a filter and controls the packets that are allowed to access and be transported through the network.[8],[9],[10] CERT is also developing a collection of network IDS signatures – patterns that identify potentially harmful service requests – based on mining historical attack logistics and the unique characteristics of previously identified threats. These signatures will be used by EINSTEIN to detect threats and inform the relevant authority.[11]

The Federal Information Security Management Act (FISMA) requires that all government agencies put into action a risk management plan to protect the information assets and systems operated by them. This process also includes frequent auditing and reviewing by the heads of these agencies to ensure compliance and to stay on top of rising security risks. The National Institute of Standards and Technology (NIST) has outlined a set of steps for ensuring compliance with the FISMA. This includes thoroughly analyzing the information assets to be protected, design and refinement of controls, testing and implementation of controls followed by constant monitoring.

The Computer Fraud and Abuse Act was written with the intention to prohibit access to computers meant for use by the departments or agencies of the U.S. However, this law has been criticized for being too broad and outdated.[12] Currently an amendment called 'Aaron's Law' has been proposed, in honor of Aaron Swartz.[13]

The risks posed by the personnel working in the federal offices has been mitigated by policies for thorough background checks performed on individuals who are employed at these offices, selective information disclosure based on rank of the individual and thorough screening of outside individuals who need to enter the premises.

Recommendations for Greater Resiliency
People and ignorance about the potential areas of risk are a major cause for IT risks, particularly security-related ones. Training and education can be effective in mitigating a large number of these threats. Legislation that mandates training with respect to the dos and don'ts of IT systems as a part of induction

programs for all companies and industries would be a good way to reach out to more people. Education regarding the ethical and safe use of IT must also be made a part of high school curriculum. On the government side, processes for increased security must be established, both physical and cyber.

Operational Risks in IT – The Private Sector

In the private sector, IT risks influence not only the company's business and the economy, but in extreme cases can even threaten the security of the nation. There are two aspects to security related risks. Risks that effect the functioning of the business processes and security risks that affect the privacy of consumers.

For online retail giants the operational risks are largely in the systems and processes domain. These organizations are known to store large volumes of data related to customer and vendor information, transaction histories, supply chain information, and inventory information in data warehouses. These information objects are critical to the functioning of the business. The information systems that handle all these processes must be infallible. Any errors in processing, particularly transaction and inventory processing can lead to grave economic losses. Other system risks include the breakdown of the key non-functional requirements of such systems - availability, reliability, and recovery.

Data is one of the most important assets of an organization. A number of factors contribute to the risk of data loss – breakdown of servers, operating systems and application software; natural disasters like earthquakes and hurricanes; physical damage to the data stores as a result of electric circuit malfunctions due to power surges or faulty communication infrastructure; and accidental misplacement of laptops and storage systems like USB memory cards. Apart from processing data such as transaction information, the work performed by employees on a daily basis is also liable to loss. This could be because of inadequate saving processes, accidental overwriting, and so on.

To protect against the risk of data loss, companies maintain redundant data stores. Geographically dispersed and redundant data centers help in reducing the possibility of data loss from natural disasters and dependency on power. But on the other side, the more redundant data centers there are, the more vulnerable the data becomes to security threats such as physical and cyber breaches. Decisions about the number of sites and their locations must be carefully made, keeping these trade-off considerations in mind. Adequate security measures need to be instituted at each site.

There are technology specific and company culture specific risks to be considered as well. For example, businesses are now largely moving into the cloud and mobile services platform. The wireless nature of these services poses additional threats to the information. Many IT companies today follow the work from home or the 'bring your own device' program (BYOD) that allows employees to use their personal device to connect to the corporate networks and perform their tasks. This increases vulnerability of networks and data as a lot of responsibility is placed on humans – the weakest link – to safeguard the resources. Intel has a security model that includes controls such as authentication, antivirus and antimalware, restricted access to company resources, encrypted data storage.[14] They also talk about educating employees on the risks, their impact and preventive measures to be taken.[15] These are a good set of controls that companies implementing BYOD and work-from-home options can apply. The policy must also address issues such as wiping out the device in case of suspected threats and clearly identify who is responsible and accountable for the resources and their potential compromise.[16],[17]

Companies like social networking sites, online retail websites, email providers etc. provide personalized services to users by requiring them to login using unique credentials. With personalization comes the risk of identity theft, a serious operational risk faced by companies that deal with sensitive information such as addresses, credit card information and details about personal lives of the consumers are dealt with. By gaining unauthorized access to a person's profile, a cybercriminal can pose as another person to perform unlawful activities. These could range from posting inappropriate content, downloading inappropriate or unlawful information to communicating information of a threatening nature via email or chat applications. Over the past two years, there has been a rise in the number of hacking attempts made at IT organizations.[18] This is external operational threat that is rising in severity. The risk of unauthorized access is increased once again due to the weakest link in the system – the people. Employees who have the authorization to manage security firewalls are threats because they have the potential to intentionally or unintentionally open them up.

Social networking websites have additional security requirements. They must provide sufficient security options on their applications for users to moderate the content they share with different groups of people.

Companies that develop software and applications like Microsoft, Amazon etc. also face liability risks pertaining to patents and intellectual property. They also face the risk of litigation from consumers for issues such as breach of security, malfunctioning products, and so on. Failure to guard against these risks will result in economic losses and loss of brand value of the company. It could also result in loss of business opportunity due to mismanaged IT resources.

The IT sector has infrastructural dependencies on other sectors like the communications sector and the energy sector. The energy sector is the source of power and the communications sector handles the risks related to the network and Internet infrastructures. Breakdowns in either of these sectors will result in automatic breakdown of all the IT systems within the perimeter of operation of the failed energy and communication sources. These additional external risks must be accounted for in a risk assessment plan, by both the private organizations as well as the government.

Current Risk Mitigation Policies

There are a number of effective IT risk assessment frameworks and controls devised by standards organizations. These frameworks include ITIL, ISO 20000, ISO 9000, COBIT, VAL IT, and others. The frameworks provide guidelines for managing different aspects of IT risks. The VAL IT framework deals more with IT risks from the business perspective -

leveraging IT to gain competitive advantage and the various factors to consider while taking a business decision based on IT.[19]

The Risk IT framework is an extension of COBIT and VAL IT published by the ISACA in 2009.[20] It covers the entire domain of IT related risks, not just focusing on IT security.[21] The frameworks and guidelines set out by these organizations help in preparing to face IT risks.

With the recent breaches in cyber security seen in commercial organizations, federal regulation to ensure that these companies protect their information assets has gained more importance than ever before. In addition to the business risks associated with these kinds of breaches, they also pose a severe threat to the economy, privacy of citizens and national security. Comprehensive federal laws to safeguard against these type of cyber threats has not been passed as yet, although legislators have been lobbying for laws such as the Cyber Security Act and the CISPA. While the CISPA is still being pushed for, President Obama signed a Presidential Policy Directive that provides for sharing of cyber security related information between the private sector and the federal government in order to better protect the nation from these attacks.[22]

The National Institute of Standards and Technologies (NIST) is currently working on cyber security regulations for private businesses to use as a guideline in order to ensure security of their critical resources.[23] They have also published a set of controls for the different nuances of information security, such as the NIST Special Publication 800 30.

Recommendations for Greater Resiliency in the Private Sector

The security of the system needs to be frequently updated. Cyber threat is an entirely different league of security threats. Safeguarding against these requires specialized knowledge and tools. Every company that uses IT must recruit specialists in IT security, or outsource it to a security management firm. In either case, the IT risk control policies must be framed very specific to the operations of that company. While COSO and COBIT are excellent frameworks for framing these policies, the companies and their security partners must go beyond them and analyze the specific situation inherent in the company. COSO and COBIT can be treated as a basic requirement with which organizations must comply.

Despite being aware of the threats, many companies do not strictly enforce prevention measures, especially at the individual employee level. Employees might cancel processes such as automatically scheduled machine scans and updates if this happens to interfere with their normal working. Regular maintenance of the servers and workstations, and power backup utilities has become more important than before. Exercising effective controls and strict vigilance at every level will go a long way in building resilience.

The potency of IT risks needs to be recognized at the top level. They need to be considered at the same level as market risks, credit risks and so on by the top management.[24] IT risks are often relegated to lower level team leaders or project managers. With the increase in the number of attacks in the recent past, companies must recognize the need to integrate solutions for IT risks within the overall risk management framework of the company, and consider these risks while making business decisions such as investing in a novel technology. This recommendation is in accordance with the guidelines outlined in the Risk IT framework. [25]

The security assurance plans must span the entire lifecycle of the information asset. Security must be a priority that is monitored from the beginning stages to the stage when the system is decommissioned or disposed of. Responsible management of decommissioned systems and the information that they contain must be outlined in the risk assessment plan. This holds good for the government side as well as the private sector.

Implementing the recommended measures in addition to following the well established guidelines of standards organizations such as ISACA and NIST will take the nation a step forward in building a more resilient future on the IT side.

---

[1] "IT risk assessment frameworks: real-world experience" *CSO Online*. Accessed 8 May 2013 <www.csoonline.com>.

[2] "Factor analysis of information risk" Wikipedia. Accessed 8 May 2013 <www.wikipedia.org>.

[3] "Cyber-security regulation" Wikipedia. Accessed 8 May 2013 <wwww.wikipedia.org>

[4] "National Cyber Security Division" Wikipedia. Accessed 8 May 2013 <www.wikipedia.org>

[5] "What is EINSTEIN" *TechTarget*. Apr 2010. Accessed 8 May 2013 <www.searchsecurity.techtarget.com>

[6] "Privacy Impact Assessment EINSTEIN Program" U.S. Department of Homeland Security. Sep 2010. Accessed 8 May 2013 <www.dhs.gov>.

[7] Wikipedia. "Einstein (U.S.-CERT program)" Wikipedia. Accessed 8 May 2013.

[8] TechTarget.com.

[9] DHS.

[10] Wikipedia, "Einstein (U.S.-CERT program)".

[11] Ibid.

[12] "The Law Used To Target Aaron Swartz Doesn't Make Sense Anymore" *Business Insider*. 20 Jan. 2013. Accessed 8 May 2013 <www.businessinsider.com>.

[13] Ibid.

[14] "Five Steps to Consumerization of IT" Intel. Oct 2012. Accessed 8 May 2013 <www.intel.com>.

[15] Ibid.

[16] Ibid.

[17] Subramaniam, Rajesh. *BYOD: Organizational Impacts of Mobile Computing and Convergence.* The ASA Institute for Risk and Innovation. Nov. 2012. Accessed 8 May 2013 <www.anniesearle.com>.

[18] Luco, Devin. *Malware Analysis: A Look Into the Past and Future.* The ASA Institute for Risk and Innovation. Nov. 2012. Accessed 8 May 2013 <www.anniesearle.com>.

[19] *Val IT Framework for Business Technology Management.* Information Systems Audit and Control Association. Accessed 8 May 2013 <www.isca.org>.

[20] *Risk Framework for Management of IT Related Business Risks.* Information Systems Audit and Control Association. Accessed 8 May 2013 <www.isca.org>.

[21] Ibid.

[22] Fact Sheet: Presidential Policy Directive on Critical Infrastructure Security and Resilience. The White House. 12 Feb. 2013. Accessed 8 May 2013 <www.whitehouse.gov>.

[23] "NIST Drafting Private Sector Cyber Framework; Ari Schwartz Comments" *ExecutiveGov*, Executive Mosaic. 13 Mar 2013. Accessed 8 May 2013 <www.executivegov.com>.

[24] Risk Framework.

[25] Risk Framework.

The Art of Social Engineering

Devin Luco
April 2013

Abstract – *Do you know all your coworkers? All the people who work in your building? Do you ask for identification or verification each time you receive a request for information? All too often, the answer to these types of questions is "no," and this opens up organizations and individuals alike to the threat of social engineering attacks. Devin defines social engineering and discusses how it negatively affects organizations. It also provides recommendations on how to defend and protect against attackers using social engineering techniques.*

Introduction

In today's information age, cyber threats are very real and will continue to be a concern for organizations. Cyber threats expose vulnerabilities in an organization's security infrastructure to gain valuable information, usually for financial gain. Cyber-attacks can cause system disturbance and uncover information such as credit card numbers, passwords, and proprietary documents that can cost individuals and organizations from hundreds to billions of dollars. Sometimes cyber-attacks are motivated by a personal vendetta or retaliation. For example, in late

March 2013, a Dutch-firm retaliated with a global
denial-of-service attack that caused a web disruption
for millions of users after the company was placed on
an anti-spam blacklist.[1] Regardless of the motivation,
not all threats are considered technical or require
expert knowledge in a particular coding program. In
fact, a very popular threat that is used by cyber
criminals is one that is non-technical and more so
psychological. This form of security threat is one that
plays on the emotions of humans and takes advantage
of our natural desire to be trusting. According to
Forbes.com, the number one security threat of 2013
that has been identified: *social engineering.*[2]

What is Social Engineering?

There are different ways to define social engineering.
The following definition of social engineering was
given to IT professionals during a 2011 global survey:[3]

*"Social Engineering is the act of breaking corporate
security by manipulating employees into divulging
confidential information. It uses psychological tricks to
gain trust, rather than technical cracking techniques.
Social Engineering includes scams such as obtaining a
password by pretending to be an employee, leveraging
social media to identify new employees more easily
tricked into providing customer information, and any
other attempt to breach security by gaining trust."*[4]

The purpose of this survey, which included IT professionals in the U.S., United Kingdom, Canada, Australia, New Zealand, and Germany, was to understand the overall industry awareness of social engineering incidents and how it affects organizations.[5] The results demonstrate an issue that still plagues organizations today. The survey showed that 97 percent of security professionals were aware that social engineering is considered a threat and 43 percent of those individuals claim they or their organization have been a victim of social engineering tactics.[6] Clearly, attackers are using and will continue to use social engineering to gain valuable information from others.

Social engineers use four basic philosophies:

- Being confident and attracting attention rather than hiding and looking suspicious.[7]
- Giving you something and building trust.[8]
- Using humor as a common tool to get people's guard down.[9]
- Requesting and then providing a reason that sounds legitimate.[10]

A social engineering attack can occur at any time and any place. It does not just impact businesses but it can also impact individuals. Regardless if a potential target thinks he or she may not contain any valuable information, individuals are targeted for a reason. They have something valuable that attackers want. Criminals using social engineering techniques can gain valuable insight such as passwords, user names, addresses, phone numbers, and much more. With one small piece of information, an attacker using social engineering can create an entire portfolio on a target. Before you know it, he or she may have your entire identify to use at his or her disposal.

Impact to Organizations

What does this mean for an organization? Many organizations have security measures, such as passwords, encryptions, and locks, in place to protect company software and hardware. At the very least, many organizations use badge readers, keys, and front desk receptionists to secure entry and deter unauthorized personnel from entering.

These measures often do not protect against social engineers. For example, have you ever held a door open for someone while entering a building? Often in buildings that require an electronic key or badge to enter, criminals using social engineering tactics will wait outside until someone enters the building. At that time, he or she will ask you to hold the door open because "I forgot my badge (key) at my desk" or another reason similar to this. The natural thing to do is feel empathy and let this person in without much thought. However, this is what a social engineer is hoping will happen. Once the unauthorized person is in the building, they have access to whatever is inside and, if desired, let additional unauthorized people through the door to help with the crime. Chris Nickerson, founder of a Colorado-based security consultancy firm, states that this tactic of following others into a building is known as "tailgating."[11] Nickerson has conducted a number of security penetration tests using social engineering practices. He also states "a cigarette is a social engineer's best friend."[12] Many of his tests begin by joining a "fellow" co-worker in a common break area outside, usually a designated smoking area.[13] While Nickerson gains the trust of employees outside, he is rarely asked for identification when the break is over and it is time to enter the building. Most employees assume he is just another employee, rather than a consultant who is testing the company's security procedures.

There are other ways social engineering can harm an organization. Attackers can also use the phone as a primary means to gain information. Sal Lifrieri, a social engineering specialist for Protective Operations, describes methods social engineers use to lure targets into giving information.[14] According to Sal, social engineers learn the corporate jargon and may call posing as an employee of the same company or an authoritative organization.[15] One trick social engineers use over the phone is recording the music that is played when placed on hold.[16] This will gain the trust of the target and will be willing to provide information with little effort from the attacker.

Recommendations

Defending yourself against social engineering is not a perfect science. However, the first step to protection is awareness. Of course, being aware will not keep you safe as statistics show that most security professionals are already aware of social engineering. However, knowing how to identify what an attack looks like and being cautious will also help in your defense. For organizations, conducting and keeping up-to-date awareness training for employees will be essential for security.[17] Lifrieri states in his trainings "…you always need to be slightly paranoid and anal because you never really know what a person wants out of you."[18] This attitude will need to be reiterated in staff awareness trainings to form an understanding that security is important.

In addition to awareness training, employees should always follow procedure in regards to releasing information.[19] Employees should be trained to question when someone is making a request and should not be hesitant to ask for identification. Treat the information at your organization as your own and be sure to inform a manager or supervisor when a request for information seems out of the ordinary.[20]

Continuous monitoring and testing are additional ways for an organization to fight against social engineering.[21] Monitoring company systems and conducting internal tests using social engineering strategies will reveal where a company's vulnerability points are. When vulnerabilities are identified, an organization can properly assess how a solution will be implemented.

Conclusion

Heading through the year 2013 and beyond, cyber security will continue to be a rising concern. Social engineering is considered one of the top cybersecurity threats of the year, mostly because it does not require technical knowledge. People will be targeted because human error and vulnerability is the easiest element of which to take advantage. It will be important for organizations to train employees to be aware of these attacks and be cautious when things do not feel right. There is not a perfect way to defend against this particular attack; but understanding what social engineering looks like and listening to your gut will be key in helping keep yourself and your company safe.

[1] Warman, Matt. "Web Slows Under 'Biggest Attack Ever.'" *The Telegraph*. 27
          Mar. 2013. Accessed 4 Apr. 2013 <www.telegraph.co.uk>.

[2] Teller, Tomer. "The Biggest Cybersecurity Threats of 2013." *Forbes*. 5 Dec.
          2012. Accessed 4 Apr. 2013 <www.forbes.com>.

[3] *The Risk of Social on Information Security: A Survey of IT Professionals*.
          Dimensional Research. 1 Sep. 2011. Accessed 4 Apr 2013
          <www.checkpoint.com>.

[4] Ibid.

[5] Ibid.

[6] Ibid.

[7] Goodchild, Joan. "Social Engineering: The Basics." *CSO Security and Risk*. 20
          Dec. 2012. Accessed Apr. 5 2013 <www.csoonline.com>.

[8] Ibid.

[9] Ibid.

[10] Ibid.

[11] Ibid.

[12] Ibid.

[13] Ibid.

[14] Ibid.

[15] Ibid.

[16] Ibid.

[17] Ibid.

[18] Ibid.

[19] Olavsrud, Thor. "9 Best Defenses Against Social Engineering Attacks."
          eSecurity Planet. 19 Oct. 2010. Accessed 6 Apr. 2013
          <www.esecurityplanet.com>.

[20] Olavsrud, Thor.

[21] "Five Ways to Protect Your Organization Against Social Engineering." *IT
          Business Edge*. 2012. Accessed 6 Apr 2013
          <www.itbusinessedge.com>.

What is Big Data?

Devin Luco
December 2012

Abstract – *Devin takes a look at "Big Data" and discusses the challenges organizations are facing with the increasing amounts of data being created each day. Not only is data volume increasing at rapid rates, but also the velocity at which companies need to manage data and the variety of sources from which companies can access data are rising concerns. Devin also discusses why companies should utilize Big Data and provides examples of ways companies have optimized the analysis of this data to form a competitive advantage. Finally, this note concludes with takeaways that CIOs should consider when addressing the growing trend of Big Data.*

Introduction

It is no secret that technology has made tremendous strides over the past several years. As we examine the past decade, we can physically see the advancements we have made through the development and commercialization of MP3 players, smartphones, and tablets. With these new tools at our disposal, the availability and speed with which we can send and receive information is increasing at unimaginable rates. For example, who would have thought twenty years ago that we would be able to read "tweets" from our favorite football players or be able to post "status updates" about our daily lives for the world to see?

In the most recent years, we have also seen advancements in the Internet through the rise of social media and search engines. However, these advancements in technology are accompanied with new economic effects and implications. We, as technology users, are sending and receiving information through mediums such as Twitter, Facebook, and Google Search with tools such as smartphones and tablets. This has flooded the databases of most organizations and has caused concern for professionals who struggle to compile, analyze, and make informed decisions from the data that is being produced. Data scientists and engineers have coined the term "Big Data" to describe this phenomenon of large growth in data.

What is Big Data?

Although much has been talked about Big Data in the past several years, it became the buzzword of 2012. So, what exactly is big data? Organizations are still trying to grasp this concept, but more importantly, they are trying to find ways on how to manage it. According to Mandeep Khera, chief marketing officer of LogLogic, "most of them are concerned about big data, yet they don't understand what it means."[1] He continues, "Because there's been so much said about big data, there's no clear definition and everyone is confused."[2] It is true that if one were to enter "Big Data" in a search engine, such as Google or Bing, there would be numerous articles struggling to explain the concept. Moreover, most of the recent articles written describe the challenges organizations face to manage Big Data but fail to thoroughly define the term. However, organizations must first understand the subject before they can successfully manage it.

Big Data refers to a collection of large and complex data sets that becomes too difficult to store, process, and manage using established database management tools.[3] Traditionally, database management tools, such as relational databases, could be used to search and query structured data to collect information in a short period. An example of structured data is data stored in a spreadsheet. The organization of data in a spreadsheet makes it possible to quickly search using simple algorithms or functions. However, with vast amounts of data being produced through popular technologies such as social media, the amount of unstructured data has become excessive to the point where traditional database tools are ineffective. Unstructured data does not have the same organizational data types and rules that structured data has, which results in difficulty understanding where that data is stored.[4] Additionally, unstructured data is often generated through audio, video, graphical, and social media messages.[5]

Characteristics of Big Data

Approximately ten years ago Meta Group analyst Doug Laney was the first to identify the increasing data management difficulties that companies were facing.[6] Laney developed a framework, which is still used today as the industry standard, to categorize and define big data.[7] The three characteristics that form Big Data include volume, velocity, and variety.

Volume – In 2012, 2.5 billion gigabytes of data are created each day with predictions of that number doubling about every 40 months.[8] To put this into perspective, most of the advertised personal computers available, from retailers such as Best Buy, can store between 500 and 1000 gigabytes of data. Companies, more so than ever, now have massive amounts of data at their disposal for analysis, research, and business trend predictions. For example, Wal-Mart gathers 2.5 million gigabytes every hour from customer transactions.[9]

Velocity – This designation refers not only to the speed of data production but also to the speed of data processing in order to keep up with day-to-day operations.[10] Companies that rely on real-time and near real-time data can reap the benefits of a competitive advantage if they are able to process data fast enough.[11] For example, with real-time mobile GPS data, figuring out how many people are in the parking lot before the store is opened and the transactions are recorded can derive sales predictions.[12] This will provide analysts and managers with the real-time information they need to make informed and timely decisions.

Variety – According to Clive Longbottom, a research analyst for Quocirca, "the most important V is variety – if you cannot deal with a variety of streams coming through, you're not doing Big Data."[13] Big Data takes the shape of many forms including, social media messages, updates, images, and videos.[14] It also includes data collected from sensors and location signals from mobile devices.[15] In this digital age, data is being generated on every topic and from every different source one can think of.

Even though this definition and categorization seems simple enough, the organizational implications still sparks confusion among in professionals.

Utilizing Big Data

The major concern of organizations regarding data is that the data has become so large and complex that it has become extremely difficult to analyze and find relevant information. Some of the questions raised by organizations include:[16]

- How do we store all this data? Should we even store all of it?
- What is the most valuable information in this dataset?
- How can we find valuable information without analyzing it all?
- How can we use the information as a competitive advantage?

According to SAS, a business analytics and business software company, companies have choices on how to solve these problems. Organizations should analyze all the data they gather with the high-performance analytics tools available such as grid computing and in-database processing.[17] Another solution is to determine which data is relevant on the front end by using the analytical tools that are currently available.[18] This was not possible with relational database queries. In the past, relevance of data could only be determined once a query was initiated to search through stored data in warehouses.[19]

Although it may be overwhelming at first, there is valuable information in the large data sets that can lead to productivity and increased profits. According to a recent study conducted at the MIT Center for Digital Business, the top third industry leaders that used data to drive decisions were 5 percent more productive and 6 percent more profitable.[20] Some organizations are beginning to recognize this and are finding ways to utilize data to their advantage. For example, a U.S. airlines company that was experiencing a 5- to 10- minute gap between estimated and actual arrival time in 40 percent of its flights used the services of a provider that collects large amounts of data on flight arrival times.[21] The provider was able to help the airlines company bridge the gap by using the massive amounts of data collected to develop more accurate forecasting models.

Even the federal government has recognized the benefits of utilizing Big Data. Recently, the government launched a Big Data Research and Development Initiative to begin the development and application of Big Data technologies.[22] Big Data providers, such as HP, are looking to land contracts for projects that will help the federal government get up to speed.[23] Although the government's need to utilize Big Data is not as critical compared to the private sector, the movement towards Big Data in the private sector must be realized or else the consequences could mean losing a competitive advantage and failing altogether.

Conclusion – CIO Takeaways

Unstructured data will continue to grow rapidly as the demand and availability for sending and receiving real-time information increases. The growth will reach a point where Big Data will no longer be considered big. Instead, Big Data will become the norm[24] and companies will be expected to manage data that is large in volume, fast in velocity, and vast in variety. To conclude, there are a few important takeaways about Big Data that CIOs should consider:

All companies should begin thinking about how to utilize Big Data – In the early stages, only data-driven companies, such as Google and Yahoo, needed to understand user-generated data.[25] However, in order to stay competitive, all companies will need to be able to effectively compile, analyze, and process data to successfully cater to the needs of their customers. Analyzing data relating to customer preferences and interests can help companies better market products.

Useful data can come in all shapes and size – remember that data worth analyzing may not always be in front of you. Server logs and sensor data can offer valuable insight by tracking customer behaviors and providing frequent data feeds.[26]

You will need a Big Data specialist – this one is self-explanatory. If you are migrating to a Big Data platform or solution, you will need to find people that with expertise in analyzing data using these new systems.[27]

Delay worrying about organizing Big Data – As a rule of thumb, gather the data first, and then sort it out later. Unlike structured data and data warehouses, you do not need to know what you are looking for before you collect the data.[28]

---

[1] Olavsrud, Thor. "Big Data Causes Concern and Big Confusion." *CIO Magazine*. 24 Feb. 2012 Accessed 3 Dec. 2012 <www.cio.com>.

[2] Ibid.

[3] Savitz, Eric. "The Death of Big Data." *Forbes*. 4 Oct. 2012. Accessed 3 Dec. 2012 <www.forbes.com>.

[4] "Achieving Value From Machine- and User-Generated Unstructured Data." Database Trends and Applications. 22 Aug. 2012. Accessed 3 Dec. 2012 <www.dbta.com>.

[5] Ibid.

[6] "Big Data: Is Your Business Ready?" ITPro. 29 Oct. 2012 Accessed 3 Dec. 2012 <www.itpro.co.uk>.

[7] Ibid.

[8] McAfee, Andrew and Brynjolfsson, Erik. "Big Data: The Management Revolution." *Harvard Business Review*. 1 Oct. 2012. Accessed 3 Dec. 2012 <hbr.org>.

[9] Ibid.

[10] "Big Data."

[11] McAfee.

[12] Ibid.

[13] "Big Data."

[14] McAfee.

[15] Ibid.

[16] "Big Data – What is it?" SAS. 2012. Accessed 4 Dec. 2012 <www.sas.com>

[17] Ibid.

[18] Ibid.

[19] Ibid.

[20] McAfee.

[21] Ibid.

[22] Corbin, Kenneth. "Federal Government's Big Data Efforts Lagging." *CIO*
        Magazine. 29 Nov. 2012. Accessed 4.
Dec. 2012 <www.m.cio.com>.

[23] Ibid.

[24] Savitz.

[25] Jackon, Joab. "Five Things CIOs Should Know About Big Data." *CIO*
        Magazine. 12 May. 2012. Accessed 4. Dec. 2012 <www.m.cio.com>.

[26] Ibid.

[27] Ibid.

[28] Ibid.

Chapter V
Physical Risks

Pacific Northwest Earthquake Risk

Andrew H. R. Hansen
February 2012

Abstract – *Over the past two years, major earthquakes have devastated Haiti, Chile, and Japan. Andrew presents why the Pacific Northwest has unique geological conditions that make it susceptible to deep, shallow and megathrust earthquakes. The Seattle Fault and liquefaction pose an additional threat to the greater Seattle area. Research indicates that high building codes and warning systems can help mitigate damages and minimize casualties. Individuals and organization should research regional threats and ensure appropriate disaster recovery plans have been prepared.*

Introduction

The past two years has been witness to multiple major earthquakes that tore through Haiti, Chile, and Japan. These quakes took thousands of lives, destroyed homes, businesses and major infrastructure, and required billions of dollars in recovery costs.[1] Natives of Washington probably remember the Nisqually earthquake of 2001, a 6.8 magnitude quake that caused $2 billion in damage, more than any other event in the U.S. state's history.[2] These events stand as stark reminders of the importance of preparing crisis management, disaster recovery, or continuity plans, should a major quake hit closer to home. This research note will focus on the geological factors that make the Pacific Northwest and the West Coast particularly susceptible to earthquakes, and will then highlight precautionary efforts that have been taken to better mitigate this threat.

Earthquakes and the Pacific Northwest

To begin with, an earthquake is a "shaking of the ground caused by the sudden breaking and movement of large sections (tectonic plates) of the earth's rocky outermost crust. Most earthquakes occur along the fault lines when the plates slide past each other or collide against each other."[3] The Pacific Northwest is unique in terms of earthquake vulnerability primarily because of its geologic setting. The Cascadia Subduction zone is "a 680-mile fault that runs 50 miles off the coast of the Pacific Northwest – from Cape Mendocino in California to Vancouver Island in southern British Columbia,"[4] and is a collision of the Juan de Fuca plate, which forms the floor of the northeastern Pacific Ocean, and the North American plate.[5] The Juan de Fuca plate is sliding underneath the American Plate at an average rate of two inches per year.[6] This type of movement makes the Northwest susceptible to three different types of earthquakes: shallow, deep, and megathrust quakes.

Cascadia earthquake sources

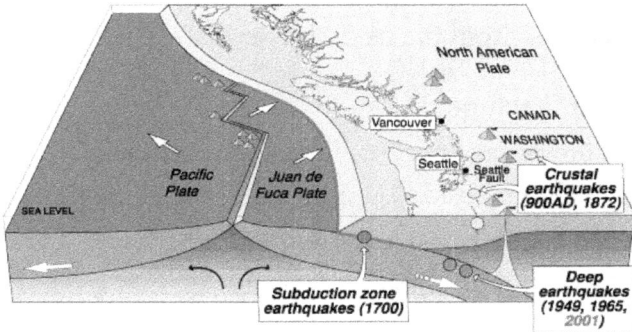

Source	Affected area	Max. Size	Recurrence
◉ Subduction Zone	W.WA, OR, CA	M 9	500-600 yr
◉ Deep Juan de Fuca plate	W.WA, OR,	M 7+	30-50 yr
○ Crustal faults	WA, OR, CA	M 7+	Hundreds of yr?

7

Deep Earthquake

The Seattle Office of Emergency Management defines deep quakes as earthquakes that occur at depths of approximately 35 to 70km.[8] "Since they are further from the surface, they are not felt as intensely, but are experienced over a wider area than shallow quakes."[9] The 2001 Nisqually earthquake was a product of movement from the Juan de Fuca plate, and is an example of a deep quake.[10] It is estimated that Juan de Fuca fault has the potential to produce an earthquake that reaches 7.5 in magnitude.[11] According to researchers with the Cascadia Region Earthquake Workgroup (CREW), there is an 84 percent chance of a magnitude 6.5 or higher deep earthquake occurring in the Puget Sound region sometime within the next 50 years.[12]

Shallow Earthquake

A shallow quake occurs at depths from zero to 30km.[13] Compared to deep or megathrust, a shallow quake may come across as sounding weak, but that is definitely not the case. Because the fault is closer to the surface, shallow quakes have the potential to cause severe damage. The 7.0 magnitude earthquake that struck near Port-au-Prince, Haiti in 2010 is an example of a shallow quake.[14] The "epicenter – the spot on a map where the earthquake occurs – was only 10 miles from Port-au-Prince… The hypocenter – the spot in the ground from which the vibrations spread – was so shallow," at only nine miles beneath the surface.[15] This quake affected 3.5 million people, injuring over 300,000 and finished with a death toll close to 220,000.[16] The fault line that caused the Haiti quake is similar in structure to the San Andreas Fault that slices through much of California.[17]

Megathrust Earthquake

A megathrust earthquake is caused by a sudden slip in a subducting and overriding plate - it represents the largest type of potential earthquake.[18] Magnitude of megathrust quakes can range from 8.0 to over 9.0 and generally occur at intervals of 200 to 1,100 years.[19] The 2011 earthquake in Japan is an example of this type of quake. The 9.0 magnitude quake "ruptured near the boundary between the Pacific and North American tectonic plates… where the Pacific plate drove underneath Japan at the Japan Trench. The seafloor was pushed away from Japan sending waves roaring toward Hawaii and the West Coast of the U.S."[20] A thirty-foot tsunami hit Japan shortly after the quake and more than 275 aftershocks of magnitude 5 or greater continued to rock the country in the days that followed.[21]

The interface between the Juan de Fuca and North American plates has the potential to slip in a similar manner.[22] In a 2010 interview, Bill Steele, the Seismology Lab Coordinator for the Pacific Northwest Seismograph Network at the University of Washington's Department of Earth and Space Sciences, described the effects of subduction zone slip in this way:

"That strain builds up until it can't stay locked together anymore, a break begins, and boom! So right away the coastline falls, the seafloor pops up and that displaces this huge column of water above there, generating a tsunami, which will affect the entire Pacific Basin if we have a magnitude 9 again."[23]

Steele went on to describe a possible megathrust quake in the Pacific Northwest in this way:

"Rather than 17 seconds or 30 seconds we're going to be dealing with ground motion running perhaps six minutes total for the rupture to occur, that starts on one end and goes to the other, and strong ground motion in our area of maybe three minutes."[24]

Based on historical averages, researchers estimate the odds of a megathrust quake occurring off the coast of the Pacific Northwest to be roughly 10 -14 percent in the next fifty years.[25]

The Seattle Fault and Liquefaction

The Seattle Fault is a crustal fault that runs east-west through Seattle from Issaquah to Bremerton and is also potentially concerning as experts speculate that it was the cause of very large earthquake approximately 1,100 years ago.[26] The Seattle Fault is complicated further by the high potential for liquefaction. Liquefaction is a term that describes how the strength and stiffness of a soil deposit are reduced because of pressure, a phenomenon most commonly induced by earthquakes.[27] Liquefaction can manifest itself in the form of landslides or by causing foundations and retaining structures to settle or tilt.[28] The SODO district of Seattle has been identified as an area that may be highly susceptible to liquefaction as it is underlain with artificial fill.[29] The King County Flood Control District labels most of South and West Seattle as areas that have high vulnerability to liquefaction.[30]

Precautions

Governments, educators, and businesses are learning the value of precautionary efforts in order to better prepare for catastrophic events. The following sections look at the ways implementing stronger building codes and utilizing warning systems can better protect and prepare the public when a natural disaster takes place.

Building Codes

The earthquakes in Chile and Haiti bring attention to the possible implication associated with better building codes. As mentioned, the Haiti earthquake registered at 7.0, while the Chile earthquake came in at 8.8.[31] Despite the fact that the Chile earthquake was more powerful, the Chilean death toll was less than 1 percent that of Haiti's.[32] This discrepancy is likely a product of multiple variables, but the "economic answer is that Chile is a modernized and industrialized nation, with a per capita economic output that's more than 10 times larger than Haiti's. As such, building codes are far stricter and better-enforced, emergency resources are more available, and the population is better educated as to the safest place to take refuge."[33] Similarly, since 2005 all Japanese buildings are required to be able to withstand a magnitude 8.0 earthquake.[34]

Warning Systems

In late 2011, the University of Washington and two other California schools were the recipients of a $6 million grant for an earthquake early warning system that would alert the public seconds to minutes before the ground starts shaking.[35] The warning systems are expensive, and some argue that they "would do Seattle little good in the case of a quake on the shallow fault that underlies the city but could benefit Olympia and other cities."[36] Perhaps this grant will lead to a system similar to that of Japan. In 2007, Japan launched the world's most sophisticated early-warning system, a nationwide online system that "detects tremors, calculates an earthquake's epicenter and sends out brief warnings from its 1,000-plus seismographs scattered throughout the country."[37] Alert messages are automatically issued via locations like factories, TV networks, radio stations, and mobile phones.[38]

Providing even a few seconds of warning would allow people time to take shelter, "prompt railroads to stop trains before they cross vulnerable bridges or even prompt physicians to stop a surgery," actions that could potentially save thousands of lives and millions of dollars.[39] An early warning might provide even more value in the event of a major quake off the coast. John Vidale, director of the Pacific Northwest Seismic Network at the University of Washington, says that an early warning system could provide Seattle with "as much as five minutes' warning of a coastal megaquake such as the one that rocked Japan and unleashed a deadly tsunami."[40] Those extra few minutes of preparation could make a dramatic difference to those scrambling to safety.

Conclusion

Discussing the probabilities of earthquakes and the damages associated with them can cause a sense of vulnerability and alarm. According to Steele:

"It's tough when you say it could be centuries before it happens or it could be tomorrow. That's an awful big window for people to get their arms around, right? Should I be totally panicked or not care at all? What we're hoping is that people find some middle ground there."[41]

Finding this "middle ground" will result in different behaviors depending on individual situations and needs. There are several resources available online, in books, or through emergency preparedness experts that can help people better understand ways to prepare homes and business to respond to emergency situations. Individuals should take the time to research threats that may be more prevalent in their specific regions and ensure that plans account for higher probability events.

Organizations will want to ensure they have a disaster recovery plan in place and that necessary precautions have been taken to protect their employees and preserve their critical assets. Individuals will also want to develop a neighborhood or family disaster plan and assemble an emergency supplies kit. As Annie Searle indicates in her book, **Advice from a Risk Detective**, "The best way to think about what goes into an emergency kit is to assume that you will not have power or grocery or medical services for three to five days."[42]

In addition, many governments and universities already have emergency warning systems in place. For example, the University of Washington has a UW Emergency Management Alert system that warns of severe weather and other alarming activities. Researching similar services that are already available in your own region will help you be better prepared and allow you to respond with more confidence.

[1] Wade, Jared. "2010 Disasters Cost the World $218 Billion and the Insurance Industry $43 Billion." *Risk Management Monitor.* 29 Mar. 2011. Accessed 8 Feb. 2012 <www.riskmanagementmonitor.com>.

[2] Meszaros, Jacqueline, and Mark Fiegener. "Effects of the 2001 Nisqually Earthquake on Small Businesses In Washington State." *Economic Development Administration, U.S. Department of Commerce.* Oct. 2002. Accessed 8 Feb. 2012 <peer.berkeley.edu>.

[3] "What is an Earthquake?" *Parenting and the Next Generation.* n. d. Accessed 8 Feb. 2012 <www.vtaide.com>.

[4] Lloyd, Robin. "Tsunami-Generating Earthquake Near U.S. Possibly Imminent." *Live Science.* 3 Jan. 2005. Accessed 8 Feb. 2012 <www.livescience.com>.

[5] "Earthquake Hazards." U.S. Geological Survey, U.S. Department of the Interior. n. d. Accessed 8 Feb. 2012 <geomaps.wr.usgs.gov>.

[6] Cole, Karen. "If Puget Sound is Falling Down." *Yahoo News.* 9 Dec. 2007. Accessed 8 Feb. 2012 <www.news.yahoo.com>.

[7] Image taken from: <www.realistnews.net/Thread-how-the-new-madrid-earthquake-might-happen-watch-for-the-events>

[8] "Earthquake." Office of Emergency Management, City of Seattle. n. d. Accessed 8 Feb. 2012 <www.seattle.gov>.

[9] "Earthquake."

[10] "The Pacific Northwest." Burke Museum of Natural History & Culture. n. d. Accessed 8 Feb. 2012 <www.burkemuseum.org>.

[11] "The Pacific Northwest."

[12] "Cascadia Deep Earthquakes." *Cascadia Region Earthquake Workgroup.* 2008. Accessed 9 Feb. 2012 <www.crew.org>.

[13] "Earthquake."

[14] Potter, Ned. "Haiti Earthquake: Why so Much Damage?" *ABC News.* 14 Jan. 2010. Accessed 8 Feb. 2012 <www.abcnews.go.com>.

[15] Potter.

[16] "Haiti Earthquake Facts and Figures." *Disasters Emergency Committee.* n. d. Accessed 8 Feb. 2012 <www.dec.org.uk>.

[17] Romero, Simon, and Marc Lacey. "Fierce Quake Devastates Haitian Capital." *The New York Times.* 12 Jan. 2010.

Accessed 8 Feb. 2012 <www.nytimes.com>.

[18] "Giant Megathrust Earthquakes." *Natural Resources Canada.* n. d. Accessed 8
        Feb. 2012 <earthquakescanada.nrcan.gc.ca>.

[19] "Earthquake."

[20] Israel, Brett. "8.9 Earthquake: The Science Behind Japan's Quake." *The
        Christian Science Monitor.* 11 Mar. 2011.
Accessed 8 Feb. 2012 <www.csmonitor.com>.

[21] MacFarlane, Jo. "And the Aftershocks go on." *Daily Mail.* 14 Mar. 2011.
        Accessed 9 Feb. 2012 <www.dailymail.co.uk>.

[22] "Earthquake."

[23] "KCTS 9 Connects." *KCTS9.* YouTube, 5 Mar. 2010. Accessed 9 Feb. 2012
        <www.youtube.com>.

[24] "KCTS 9 Connects."

[25] Steele, Bill. "Re: Annie Searle Links." Message to author. 23 May 2012. Email.

[26] Pararas-Carayannis, George. "The Earthquake of 28 Feb. 2001 in the State of
        Washington, U.S." *Disaster Page.* n.d. Accessed 9 Feb. 2012
        <www.drgeorgepc.com>.

[27] Kramer, Steven L. "Evaluation of Liquefaction Hazards in Washington State."
        *University of Washington and the Washington State Department of
        Transportation.* Dec. 2008. Accessed 9 Feb. 2012
        <www.wsdot.wa.gov>.

[28] Kramer.

[29] Kramer.

[30] "Map 11-5 Liquefaction Susceptibility." *King County Flood Control District.* n.
        d. Accessed 9 Feb. 2012 <kingcounty.gov>.

[31] Lafsky, Melissa. "The Power of Building Codes: Chile Death Toll Less Than 1
        percent of Haiti." *Infrastructurist.* 1 Mar. 2010. Accessed 9 Feb. 2012
        <www.infrastructurist.com>.

[32] Lafsky.

[33] Lafsky.

[34] Bolonos, Elly T. and Justin K. Vestil. "Buildings Built After 2005 'can
        Withstand' Magnitude 8 Quakes." *SunStar.* 9 Feb. 2012. Accessed 9
        Feb. 2012 <www.sunstar.com>.

[35] Sunde, Scott. "New Sensors may Lead to Earthquake-warning System." *SeattlePI*. 20 Nov. 2011. Accessed 9 Feb. 2012 <www.seattlepi.com>.

[36] Doughton, Sandi. "Warning System Worked, but is it Worth the Cost?" *Seattle Times*. 13 Mar. 2011. Accessed 9 Feb. 2012 <www.seattletimes.com>.

[37] Birmingham, Lucy. "Japan's Earthquake Warning System Explained." *Time Magazine*. 18 Mar. 2011. Accessed 9 Feb. 2012 <www.time.com>.

[38] Birmingham.

[39] Sunde.

[40] Doughton.

[41] "KCTS 9 Connects."

[42] Searle, Annie. *Advice From A Risk Detective*. 2011.

Violence in the Workplace

Devin Luco
January 2013

Abstract – *Far too often when we turn on the news, we hear stories of tragic violence in schools, office spaces, public spaces, and homes. Devin tackles the difficult topic of workplace violence in the wake of the Newton, Connecticut school shooting. However, not every act of violence starts with a shooting rampage, and Devin discusses ways to identify early warning signs. Identifying early warning signs of violent acts can help prepare workers and allow them to report concerns before it becomes too late. This note also discusses ways that employers and employees can protect themselves from workplace violence.*

Introduction

A little less than a month ago, the U.S. witnessed the very tragic events that took place in the suburban town of Newton, Connecticut, in which a 20-year old gunman entered and opened fire in an elementary school killing 26 people.[1] The age of the victims ranged from 6 to 56 years old, including 20 students, the school principal, psychologist, teacher and substitute teacher.[2] This traumatic event takes place

just five years after the Virginia Tech shootings where
a student killed 33 people across campus, known as
the deadliest campus shooting in U.S. history.[3] In the
aftermath of these events, very controversial issues
have been intensely debated. The hottest topic among
politicians and legislative parties is gun control in the
U.S. While lawmakers are determining regulations
around gun accessibility, we will take a closer look at a
different topic that these deadly events touch on:
violence in the workplace.

During the Connecticut shooting, one teacher,
Victoria Soto, bravely guided her students into a
closet and tried to shield them from the assailant.[4]
Soto will forever be remembered as a hero that gave
her life to protect her students. However, it is
understood that no one should ever have to make that
kind of decision, especially at work. Soto, along with
other faculty members of Sandy Hook Elementary
School, came into work that day not expecting to face
a life or death situation. This is the expectation we
should all have as employees. Despite this
expectation, many Americans may not have
confidence that employers are keeping them safe at
work. In a nationwide phone survey conducted by
David Michaelson and Company results revealed that
34 percent, of the 1,030 adults asked, go to work
afraid.[5] Based on these statistics, it is apparent that

workplace violence is a concern that needs to be addressed. At the very least employees should be aware of what workplace violence looks like, how to identify the early warning signs that may lead to workplace violence and how to protect against it.

What is Workplace Violence?

Workplace violence does not only refer to fatal or life threatening occurrences. In fact, the Occupational Safety and Health Administration (OSHA) includes physical violence, harassment, intimidation, and other threatening behaviors in its' definition of workplace violence.[6] This means that workplace violence can range from a manager verbally abusing an employee to a visitor or employee committing murder. According to OSHA, homicide is the "fourth-leading cause of fatal occupational injuries in the U.S."[7] However, many other nonfatal occupational injuries take place. A special report released in March 2011 by the U.S. Department of Justice states that in 2009 approximately 572,000 nonfatal violent incidents occurred at the workplace.[8] These nonfatal violent crimes include rape, sexual assault, robbery, and aggravated assault. Since 1993, nonfatal violent crimes have declined drastically. In 1993, nonfatal workplace violence occurrences were at 16 per 1,000 employed persons.[9] By 2009, that rate dropped to four per 1,000 employed persons.[10] In that same year, there were 521 workplace homicides.[11] As you can see, most workplace violence incidents are nonfatal. Furthermore, it is wise to assume that some nonfatal workplace violence occurrences are not reported. This can be due to a variety of reasons. Reasons to not report may include lack of proof, fear of retaliation, or even a lack of awareness that the situation is considered workplace violence. In any case, it is important to understand workplace violence, both fatal and nonfatal. The first step to protection is being able to recognize the early warning signs that workplace violence may occur.

Warning Signs of Workplace Violence

Although we can never be 100 percent safe in the workplace, or anywhere for that matter, there are early warning signs that can help us identify tensions that may lead to violent acts in the workplace. Michael Staver, a corporate and executive coach and former psychologist in a mental hospital, describes violence escalation into three stages: a trigger event, emotion escalation, and finally the violent act.[12] According to Staver, these stages can occur very rapidly or take a longer time to develop.[13] The following are Staver's early warning signs to look for:

"Excessive complaining or whining" – this may be a sign that an employee has experienced a trigger event, even more so if the worker is usually even-tempered.[14]

"Withdrawal" – Someone that avoids social contact and becomes isolated could signal having a difficult time handling a certain situation at home or work.[15]

"Variation from typical behavior" – Take notice of co-workers that are usually extroverted that suddenly become reserved and unsocial; and vice versa, look for introverts that suddenly become extroverts.[16]

"Obsessive thought patterns or conversations" – Do not dismiss the signs if an employee is constantly raving about how life is not fair and how they deserve more.[17]

"Dramatic and unreasonable demands" – Being impatient and requesting immediate assistance on situations that take a while to handle.[18]

"Personal insults" – Angry outbursts and verbally abusive co-workers could indicate that a deeper tension is developing.[19]

"Threats" – Finally, the most dangerous and apparent sign is when an employee makes verbal threats to harm someone.[20]

Of course this list is not all-inclusive, nor does it mean if an employee demonstrates these behaviors that he or she will commit a violent act. However, Staver's early warning signs does provide us with a way of being alert at the workplace and also helps us identify something may be wrong before it becomes too late.

How to Protect Against Workplace Violence?

The first step to being protected against any kind of violence is being aware and alert. In additional to learning the early warning signs, OSHA has a helpful worksheet, on its "Workplace Violence" website, that gives employers tips on best practices for protecting employees. The worksheet also gives tips for employees on how to protect themselves.

For employers:

- Provide safety training and education to employees.[21]
- Make sure the workplace is secure with video surveillance, alarm systems, security badges, and security guards.[22]
- Provide employees with cellular devices or allow them to bring devices from home to use in case of an emergency.[23]

For employees:

- Communicate with managers and human resources when safety concerns arise. Make sure to report any incidents immediately.[24]

- Refrain from entering locations where you feel unsafe or go with another co-worker if this situation is unavoidable.[25]

Many companies use a variety of the tips described above. Retail stores may have security guards roaming the store or walking around outside the premises to deter unwanted visitors. Large corporations, such as Boeing and Microsoft, require employees to use badge readers to enter buildings. Along with this, companies will regularly remind employees to watch out for "tailgaters." Tailgaters are people that pretend to be employees and access a secure building by following an actual employee through the doors. Tailgaters will also take advantage of an employee's good nature by asking them to hold the door for them thus never actually having to use a badge to enter the building. This is not only dangerous to the company but also dangerous to employees, as someone could be entering the building to commit a violent act. The best solution to this problem is to remind employees to always ask for a badge and making sure the door is closed behind them.

In addition to OSHA's guidelines, employers can offer health evaluations and stress management services that can help detect and manage risk factors before a violent act happens. Another way to be protected is keeping open communications with employees and managers. Employees must be confident enough to voice concerns and report any incidents to managers. Finally, to keep the workplace safe you can also require background checks on all employees before they are hired. Employers can discover pertinent information on potential employees such as any violent crimes on their record, especially crimes involving domestic violence.

Conclusion

Workplace violence refers to both fatal and nonfatal violent crimes. This includes but not limited to homicide, sexual assault, armed robbery, verbal abuse, and aggravated assault. Most workplace violence is of the nonfatal nature, however, due to the severity of fatal incidents we focus more on these situations. It is important for employers and employees to be aware of the early warning signs of workplace violence in order to protect themselves as well as others. There are useful guidelines that some companies are already using in order to keep the work environment safe. Although, there is no such thing as a 100 percent safe work environment, we can take certain steps and precautions to keep ourselves as safe as possible.

---

[1] Candiotti, Susan and Ford, Dana. "Connecticut School Victims Were Shot Multiple Times." *CNN.com.* 15 Dec. 2012. Accessed 5 Jan. 2013 <www.cnn.com>.

[2] Candiotti.

[3] Hauser, Christine and O'Connor, Anahad. "Virginia Tech Shooting Leaves 33 Dead." *The New York Times*. 16 Apr. 2007. Accessed 5 Jan. 2013 <www.nytimes.com>.

[4] Connor, Tracy, Lilley, Sandra, and Winter, Tom. "'Light Amidst The Darkness': Heroic Teacher Victoria Soto Remembered." *NBC News*. 19 Dec. 2012. Accessed 8 Jan. 2013 <www.nbcnews.com>.

[5] Goodchild, Joan. "Making the Case for Preventing Workplace Violence." *CSO Online*. 20 Mar. 2012. Accessed 8 Jan 2013. <m.csoonline.com>

[6] "Workplace Violence." Occupational Safety & Health Administration, U.S. Department of Labor. Accessed 8 Jan. 2013 <www.osha.gov>.

[7] Ibid.

[8] "Workplace Violence, 1993-2009." Bureau of Justice Statistics, U.S. Office of Justice Program. Mar 2011. Accessed 8 Jan 2013 <www.bjs.gov>.

[9] Ibid.

[10] Ibid.

[11] Ibid.

[12] Adams, Susan. "What Are The Signs Of Workplace Violence?" *Forbes*. 8 Mar. 2012. Accessed 9 Jan. 2013 <www.forbes.com>.

[13] Ibid.

[14] Ibid.

[15] Ibid.

[16] Ibid.

[17] Ibid.

[18] Ibid.

[19] Ibid.

[20] Ibid.

[21] "OSHA Factsheet." Occupational Safety & Health Administration, U.S. Department of Labor. Accessed 8 Jan. 2013 <www.osha.gov>.

[22] Ibid.

[23] Ibid.

[24] Ibid.

[25] Ibid.

Early Warning Detection Systems

Andrew H. R. Hansen
May 2012

Abstract – *Advances in technology have greatly improved the ability to detect natural disasters through early warning detection systems. Andrew discusses system improvements associated with fire, flood, and earthquakes, and recommends ways risk managers can improve risk preparedness plans. Andrew also touches on the growing role of social media as a tool for communicating information during a crisis.*

Introduction

As implied by the name, early warning detection systems are tools used by governments and private organizations to communicate a potential or impending problem before the event occurs.[1] Over the last two decades, technological advances have allowed researchers to dramatically improve the detection of natural disasters and provide a means to warn the public before the disaster strikes. Although the technology to predict many forms of disasters may not yet exist, the development of early warning systems that detect fires, earthquakes, floods, and other natural disasters are becoming more prominent and are appropriately credited with saving thousands of lives. This research note will analyze early warning systems associated with wildfire, floods, and earthquakes and discuss ways organizations and governments can utilize these systems to improve their emergency preparedness plans.

Wildfire

Each year in the U.S., more than 100,000 wildfires completely clear four to five million acres of land.2 Recent years have been even more damaging, with up to nine million acres of land being burned.3 Due to several environmental factors, detecting forest fires and the paths they may take can be a difficult undertaking. But researchers with Edith Cowan University's Centre for Communications Engineering Research are hoping to change that in the near future by "deploy(ing) a large test of wireless sensors that detect forest fires and broadcast the results to the world."4

The system works by utilizing proprietary mesh networking software, connected to palm-sized sensors scattered throughout the forest and connected to a wireless network.5 The sensors can "detect carbon monoxide and carbon dioxide levels found in forest fires… [and] broadcast findings to researchers or the general public via Twitter or on the Internet."6 Current remote sensors have a line of site capability of 500 feet, and have the ability to "detect up to 16 different types of environmental factors, including gas levels, atmospheric pressure, humidity and temperature."[7] Small trials of the system have been successfully conducted in highly controlled environments, but researchers are looking to deploy larger tests in the future to get a better sense of the system's capabilities and limitations.[8]

A wildfire may seem unlikely to those in urban environments, but risk managers must consider and be prepared for the threat of fires. Fire drills and evacuation should be held at least once a year.[9] In addition, professionals recommend10 employees know how to:

- Activate the fire alarm if they discover a fire
- Contact the fire department
- Use fire-fighting equipment appropriate for the circumstances
- How to evacuate the building
- Where to assemble and who to report to

Floods
Floods are characterized by having "more water flowing through the hydrological system than the system can draw off."[11] From a risk management perspective, it is important to make the distinction between a regular river flood, where water slowly raises over the edge; and a flash flood, when a wall of water quickly sweeps over an area.[12] "Almost three-

quarters of the approximately 92 deaths from floods each year are due to flash floods."[13] Unlike some natural disasters that are nearly impossible to predict, improving weather forecasting tools are enhancing the ability to predict floods.

Dual-Polarization Radar

The National Weather Service (NWS) recently upgraded Doppler technology to include a tool called dual polarization. As seen in the image to the right,[14] dual polarization allows Doppler to transmit and receive information from the atmosphere both horizontally and vertically; consequently, the ability to predict precipitation types and estimates will become more accurate.[15] All 160 NWS offices should have this new technology installed by the end of 2013.[16]

Receiving extreme weather alerts through television and radio is not a new phenomenon; however, several applications for mobile phones are now conveniently accessible through multiple mobile platforms and enable extreme weather notifications to be easily delivered to mobile devices. In addition, a highly sophisticated prototype for a flood early warning system developed by a global community of researchers:

"Monitors sensor networks installed in flood defenses (dikes, dams, embankments, etc.), detects sensor signal abnormalities, calculates dike failure probability, and simulates possible scenarios of dike breaches and flood propagation."[17]

The relevant information gathered from these sensors is then sent to a decision support system, where managers can analyze the data and make decisions that are more informed.[18]

From a risk management perspective, it is critical to identify the types of flood risks an organization or municipality is exposed to, and prepare a flood mitigation plan. Taken from the Environment Agency (EA),[19] a flood plan for a business should consist of:

- A list of important contacts, building services, suppliers and evacuation contacts for staff.
- A description or map showing locations of key property, protective materials, and service shut-off points.
- Basic strategies for protecting property, preventing business disruption and assisting recovery.

- Checklists of procedures that can be quickly accessed by staff during a flood.

The EA also correctly points out that if a flood is imminent, the primary concern should be the safety of the staff.[20]

Earthquakes

As discussed in a previous research note, earthquakes are caused "by the sudden breaking and movement of large sections (tectonic plates) of the earth's rocky outermost crust."[21] The extreme strength of two massive moving plates causes the crust to rupture at its weakest point.[22] When an earthquake occurs, waves of energy caused by the sudden breaking of rock travel through the earth and are recorded on seismographs.[23] Although earthquakes produce multiple types of measurable waves, early detection warning systems are largely interested in primary and secondary waves.

A primary wave (also referred to as a P wave, pressure wave or compressional wave) is the fastest kind of seismic wave and has the ability to move through solid rock and fluids, pushing and pulling through the earth in a similar way that sound waves push and pull through the air.[24] "Depending on the magnitude and the composition of the ground layers the P wave generally travels somewhere between 4 to 8 km/second."[25] A secondary wave (also referred to as S wave or shear wave) is "slower than a P wave and can only move through solid rock, not through any liquid medium."[26] S waves travel at approximately sixty percent[27] of the speed of the P wave and are the waves responsible for the majority of the strong shaking felt in a quake, as they "move rock particles up and down or side to side." [28]

Early warning detection systems are able to identify the faster traveling P waves and provide an advance notice of the heavy shaking that will come with the trailing S waves. As soon as the P waves are detected, data is gathered and processed and alerts are sent via television, radio, the Internet and mobile phones. The amount of warning the systems are able to provide depends upon the location relative to the epicenter of the quake. "Communities closest to the epicenter will receive no warning because they fall within what is known as the 'blind zone.'"[29] But communities further from the epicenter may receive "tens of seconds to more than a minute of warning time, but they are also less likely to experience damage from the shaking."[30] A few seconds warning may not sound like a consequential figure, "but for areas about to be rocked by seismic waves, those seconds can give emergency managers and the public just enough time to prepare and perform life-saving tasks, as well as trigger automated systems designed for such a situation."[31]

Despite the high monetary investment associated with early earthquake detection systems, countries around the globe have determined that the additional preparation time granted to their citizens is worth the cost.[32] An advanced system, similar to Japan's, has been planned for the Bay Area in northern California and along the west coast of the U.S., but has "languished for more than five years, stuck in a perpetual test phase because of a lack of government funding."[33] A recent grant of $6 million dollars should help the project progress, but officials close to the project say much more funding will be needed.[34]

As discussed earlier, the seconds to minutes of advanced warning provided by these systems can actually provide enough time to take significant safety measures. Summarized from research[35] conducted by Richard Allen of the University of California, Berkeley, the following suggestions illustrate possible ways governments and organizations could utilize the advanced warning systems:

- Trains could be slowed or stopped and positioned to avoid bridges or tunnels
- Airplanes on final approach could be issued "go around" commands

- Streetlights could be turned red – preventing cars from entering hazardous structures like tunnels or bridges
- Workers in hazardous environments could move to pre-determined safe zones
- Sensitive equipment could be automated to be put in a holding mode, limiting the risk of injury or damage
- Office workers and school children could get under desks before the shaking arrives

Conclusion

As risk managers consider the threat posed by each of these natural disasters, it is important to understand that the circumstances of each individual organization or community are going to be unique. As technology continues to improve the functionality of various early detection systems, the ways in which these systems can positively impact and improve safety will also increase. Organizations should take the time to research existing warning systems in their own communities, many of them are public services and provided at no cost. Many universities and private organizations also provide different types of warnings systems that should also be considered for inclusion in disaster preparedness planning.

In addition, both public and private organizations should not be afraid to utilize social networking tools as part of their disaster preparedness plans. Following a 2011 fire that swept through a small Canadian city, officials commented, "the fire was moving so fast it was impossible to issue a bulletin through their public warning system."[36] In the aftermath of the fire, they learned that information was not being received through traditional channels like television, radio, or mobile phone, but that people were constantly checking Facebook.[37] Social networking should not be the only means of crisis communication, but it should be considered for inclusion as one tool in a larger toolkit.

---

[1] "Toward the Development of Disease Early Warning Systems." *The National Academies Press*. n.d. Accessed 9 May 2012 <www.nap.edu>.

[2] 'Wildfires: Dry, Hot, and Windy." *National Geographic*. n.d. Accessed 9 May 2012 <environment.nationalgeographic.com>

[3] Ibid.

[4] Collins, Hilton. "Wi-Fi Network Could Help Detect Forest Fires." *Emergency Management Magazine*. 10 May 2012. Accessed 11 May 2012 <www.emergencymgmt.com>.

[5] Ibid.

[6] Ibid.

[7] Ibid.

[8] Ibid.

[9] Ibid.

[10] Adapted from "Fire Safety In the Workplace." *Gov.UK*. n.d. Accessed 10 May 2012 <www.gov.uk>.

[11] "The Hows and Whys of Floods." *Public Broadcast Service.* n.d. Accessed 10 May 2012 <www.pbs.org>.

[12] Ibid.

[13] Ibid.

[14] Image taken from: earthsky.org/earth/nws-upgrades-to-dual-polarization-radar-for-better-look-at-   precipitation-tornadoes

[15] Daniel, Matt. "NWS Upgrades to Dual-Polarization Radar for Better Look at Precipitation, Tornadoes." *Earthsky.com.* 10 Feb. 2012. Accessed 10 May 2012 <earthsky.org>

[16] Ibid.

[17] V.V. Krzhizhanovskayaa et. al. "Flood Early Warning System: Design, Implementation and Computational Modules." *Science Direct.* May 2011 <www.sciencedirect.com>.

[18] Ibid.

[19] "Prepare a Flood Plan for Your Business." *Environmental Agency.* n.d. Accessed 10 May 2012 <www.environment-agency.gov.uk>.

[20] Ibid.

[21] "What is an Earthquake." *Parenting the Next Generation.* n.d. Accessed 10 May 2012 <www.vtaide.com>.

[22] Vervaeck, Armand. "Are Earthquake "Early Warning Systems" to be Trusted?" *Earthquake Report.* 6 Apr. 2012. Accessed 10 May 2012 <earthquake-report.com>.

[23] "What is Seismology?" Michigan Technological University. n.d. Accessed 10 May 2012 <www.geo.mtu.edu>.

[24] Ibid.

[25] Vervaeck.

[26] What is Seismology.

[27] Vervaeck.

[28] What is Seismology.

[29] Nyquist, Christina. "The USGS and Partners Work to Develop an Earthquake Early Warning System for California." U.S. Geological Survey, U.S. Department of the Interior. 17 Apr. 2012. Accessed 10 May 2012 <www.usgs.gov>.

[30] Ibid.

[31] Ibid.

[32] Ibid.

[33] Upton, John, Matt Smith. "Why California Lacks and Earthquake Warning
    System Like Mexico's." *The Bay Citizen*. 22 Mar. 2012. Accessed 11
    May 2012 <www.baycitizen.org>.

[34] Ibid.

[35] Allen, Richard. "Second Before the Big One." Seismological Laboratory,
    University of California Berkeley. Apr. 2011. Accessed 11 May 2012
    <seismo.berkeley.edu>.

[36] Davison, Janet. "Social Media: One More way to Warn of Disaster." *CBC
    News*. 25 May 2011. Accessed 11 May 2012 <www.cbc.ca>.

[37] Ibid.

Chapter VI
Policies & Governance

Crisis Management – What, Why & How?

Rajesh Subramanian

December 2012

Abstract: *Crisis Management is the systematic approach of averting an imminent crisis or managing one that has already occurred. Rajesh outlines the key crisis management tools that are the foundation of a strong crisis management plan for handling emergencies. Using the examples of Hurricane Katrina, Irene, and Sandy, Rajesh evaluates how crisis responses have evolved over the years and how learning from these events has been effectively utilized to mitigate losses and fatalities.*

Introduction

The definition of a crisis has evolved over the last century. Initially, it denoted an unstable time or state of affairs with a distinct possibility of a highly undesirable outcome or an unanticipated fruitful outcome having a progressive effect.[1] Over the years, this definition was polished to include the key words such as "unexpected," "low-probability" and "high impact."[2] The delineation of crisis was expanded in 2006 to include criminal activities like an informational and financial crisis. Moreover, this addition included a psychological aspect that stated that a crisis occurs due to the ability of the human race to sit in denial of events.[3] A more recent definition by Timothy Coombs in 2007 adds the keyword perception.[4] The reliance on technology has led to the belief that we are all well protected from all disasters and our response will be instant in case something happens.[5] This drastic development in the definition of crisis has been attributed to the dynamically progressing world that we live. Such has been the periodicity of a crisis that it is no longer considered peripheral.[6] From the Tylenol incident in 1982 to the Tsunami in Japan in March 2011, disaster has struck everybody - from individuals, corporations, and states, to an entire nation – and from which no one is immune. As the word crisis starts sub-setting different spaces with time, the current need of the hour is a plan and the understanding of skills that would assist in detecting and taking necessary steps to prevent losses from an imminent crisis.

Crisis Management – What & Why?

Organizational crisis management is a systematic endeavor by organizational members with external stakeholders to avert crises or to effectively manage those that do occur.[7] In other words, it is a chain of activities that will help impede a potentially dangerous event (having a negative impact) from occurring or achieve a seamless transition from a "critical state" to "business as usual" state. Such an action or reaction portrays the need of a flexible structure that makes it possible for decisions to be made quickly and effectively during emergencies. The British Petroleum Oil spill tragedy epitomizes a casual notion of senior management about any crisis – "rolling with the punches and hoping for the best."[8] This is not so much a model as it is making decisions in an ad hoc fashion without comprehending the possible repercussions of the actions. On the other hand, when an organization has a plan in place, there is a structure that places accountability in the hands of key individuals, permitting decisions to be made autonomously as required for each situation. Such a structure also outlines a distinct line of command reducing pressure and chaos.[9] This scheme consists of three crucial phases: pre-crisis planning, crisis handling and crisis evaluation.[10] This utilization of technology combined with a crisis management plan has enabled the discovery of early warning signals that precede a crisis which help uncover liabilities that would lead to a disaster by facilitating precautionary action to avert it before it happens.[11] When an organization has both technology tools and a good plan, an organization can shift into a crisis management mode when a crisis arises unexpectedly, as it tries to identify the optimum response to manage and prevent it from becoming a full-scale catastrophe having a large effect on the organization as well as the public.[12] Finally, the crisis evaluation stage helps appraise the organization's response and reaction to the crisis, and empower an organization with the necessary knowledge and lessons on how something similar could be averted in the future.[13]

Crisis Management Essentials

Creating a crisis management plan mandates a set of actions and reactions that can be exercised, focusing on what could happen, what will happen, and what is happening.[14] In spite of the existence of a wide-ranging crisis management frameworks and tools, below are the set of basic crisis management elements that any organization should have in its armor for its effective implementation:

Crisis Management Plan

A crisis management plan is the first step towards averting a crisis or recovering from it. The plan is an information repository that details the necessary policies and guidelines for preventing potential crises and includes different strategies and tactics on how to deal with a crisis when it occurs.[15] Moreover, a proactive strategy will not only lessen the actual damage sustained by the company, it also may enable the business to affect the public's perception of the crisis and of the organization's response.[16] In addition, these plans need to be tested periodically in order to keep up with today's dynamic environment.

Crisis Management Team

In order to execute a crisis management plan, you need a team of diverse, highly skilled, and trained individuals who can act with poise and composure when under pressure. According to Coombs, "a crisis management team is a cross-functional group of people within the organization who have been designated to handle any crisis."[17] It is the responsibility of the crisis management team to concoct and execute a plan that is both comprehensive and plausible.

Crisis Management or Emergency Operations Center

Every crisis mandates a central operational center that can control the flow of information amongst the crisis management team as well as with the media.[18] This aids in remote monitoring of systems and infrastructure before, during, and after a crisis. Microsoft's Global Security Operations Center (GSOC) is a perfect example of a central management location that meritoriously mitigated risks and communicated safety information to its employees in Japan during the 2011 tsunami.[19]

Crisis Communication Plan

Every crisis management plan should include a strategic communication plan that can provide vital information to both public as well as stakeholders about the current state of affairs during a crisis. Some steps include disseminating information via different resources (online and on social media sites) to reduce ambiguity about the event. The communication plan should send out a positive vibes about the action between taken; acknowledging the event as unfortunate and specifying how the organization is trying to recover from it. With the media hype that inflates every event, the crisis communication plan is crucial to avoid the press from filling this vacuum with flawed information.[20]

Hurricanes in U.S. – How were they handled?

The U.S. Hurricane season falls between June 1 and November 31 since these dates encompass the Atlantic tropical weather activity.[21] This shows that the U.S. coastline is a breeding ground for hurricanes during this particular time of the year. In recent times, Hurricanes Sandy, Irene, Ike and Katrina have caused devastation on a huge scale. Though hurricanes were historically felt on the southeast coast, the east coast has been hit as well in the last two years. It is vital to compare and study the preventive actions taken and the response plans as per the crisis management essentials mentioned earlier.

Hurricane Katrina

Hurricane Katrina was one of the most devastating hurricanes ever to hit the U.S., leaving millions homeless.[22] Such was the intensity of the hurricane that it was considered among the five most deadly hurricanes to ever strike the U.S.[23] Though the first 72 hours after a disaster are crucial for rescue and recovery, all plans to restore order were considered useless as soon as the hurricane hit New Orleans.[24] There was ambiguity as to who was in charge, goods and supplies that arrived in the area were not well utilized, and police seemed unwilling to coordinate and bring order to a city thrown into tumult by the hurricane. There were several examples of coordination failure during the Katrina disaster. For instance, officials acknowledged that resources on the U.S.S. Bataan, already in the Gulf of Mexico, were not effectively brought to bear.[25] Little use was made of the doctors, operating rooms, hospital beds, or ability of that ship to produce 10,000 gallons of water per day.[26] The House of Representatives report of 2006 indicates that they were four different command structures operating in the aftermath, each ignorant of the others.[27] The emergency teams in New Orleans were under-staffed, unprepared and lacked funding to exercise any plans in place.[28] Generally, response to Hurricane Katrina lacked a strong crisis management plan, communication was confounding, and the response team was shorthanded making it a prime example on how crisis management should not be handled.

Hurricane Irene

Hurricane Irene, which was the first hurricane since 1903 to have made landfall in New Jersey since 1903,[29] had a powerful impact throughout the Eastern U.S., triggering losses that ran into billions of dollars. The Obama administration learned from the Federal Emergency Management Agency (FEMA) slip-ups of the Bush Administration and took necessary precautions before the storm hit the East Coast. President Barack Obama displayed excellent leadership skills by personally ensuring that the FEMA and the state government are equipped and organized ahead of time to deal with the disaster.[30] In essence, the lessons learned from Hurricane Katrina were implemented by the FEMA and the state agencies to ensure that there was a crisis management plan for evacuation and disaster recovery headed by a strong and influential group of individuals.

Hurricane Sandy

Although Hurricane Sandy was one of the most powerful hurricanes to hit the U.S., FEMA and the state officials ensured that a continuous communication thread existed always (viz. social media and press conferences) apprising everyone affected of present nature of the storm and the dangers of wandering outside.[31] Roads, subways, and tunnels were closed which indicated that a crisis management plan was in place and implemented by New York City Mayor Bloomberg and other state officials with the support of the people.[32] A specific task list was in place that ensured quick recovery from the disaster, leaving no time and room to play the blame game. In spite of its intensity, pre-planned preparations helped moderate destruction to a certain extent, which indicates that having a plan and a communication network in place did help in mitigating the losses and fatalities of the hurricane.[33]

Conclusion

To conclude, one can say that the area of crisis management is evolving with every passing second. There is no single framework available for organizations to follow that will help concoct an immortal plan that covers every contingency. As seen here, the responses to Hurricane Sandy and Irene were far better than the one for Hurricane Katrina which points out that one can only learn from each event and prepare better by evaluating responses to these events. Finally, it is important to develop a crisis management methodology that enables an organization to be ready so that responses to such events ensure feasible business recovery.

---

[1] Fink, Steven. "Crisis Management: Planning for the Inevitable." American Management Association. 1986.

[2] Pearson, Christine M., & Judith A. Clair. "Reframing Crisis Management." Academy of Management Review. 1998.

[3] Mitroff, Ian I., Michael A. Diamond, and Murat C. Alpaslan. "How Prepared are America's Colleges and Universities for Major Crises?" *Change Magazine*: 2006.

[4] Coombs, W. Timothy. "Ongoing Crisis Communication: Planning, Managing, and Responding". Sage Publications, Inc. 2011.

[5] Ibid.

[6] Sellnow, Timothy L., Matthew W. Seeger, and Robert R. Ulmer. "Effective Crisis Communication: Moving from Crisis to Opportunity." Sage Publications, Inc. 2010.

[7] Hart, Paul, Uriel Rosenthal, and Alexander Kouzmin. "Crisis Decision Making The Centralization Thesis Revisited." *Administration & Society*. 1993. Accessed 7 Dec. 2012. <politicsir.cass.anu.edu.au>

[8] Nudell, Mayer, and Norman Antokol. "Handbook of Effective Emergency and Crisis Management." 1988.

[9] "Crisis Management – An International Overview." Hong Kong Efficiency Unit. Accessed 7 Dec. 2012 <www.eu.gov.hk>.

[10] Smith, Katelyn. "Best Practices for Effective Corporate Crisis Management: A Breakdown of Crisis Stages Through the Utilization of Case Studies." Diss. California Polytechnic State University. 2012. Accessed 7 Dec. 2012 <digitalcommons.calpoly.edu>.

[11] Mitroff, Ian I., Paul Shrivastava, and Firdaus E. Udwadia. "Effective Crisis Management." *The Academy of Management Executive (1987-1989)*. 1987. Accessed 7 Dec. 2012 <www.paulshrivastava.net>.

[12] Devlin, Edward S. "Crisis Management Planning and Execution". Auerbach Publications. 2006.

[13] Miller, Julie A. "An Empirical Study of the Effects of Perception of Corporate Crises on Crisis Management." Diss. San Diego State University. 1992.

[14] Clark, Jonathan, and Mark Harman. "On Crisis Management and Rehearsing a Plan." Risk Management-New York. 2004. Accessed 7 Dec. 2012 <www.freepatentsonline.com>.

[15] Jaques, Tony. "Issue Management As A Post-Crisis Discipline: Identifying And Responding To Issue Impacts Beyond The Crisis." *Journal of Public Affairs.* 1 Sep. 2009. Accessed 7 Dec. 2012 <www.issueoutcomes.com.au>.

[16] Miller.

[17] Coombs.

[18] Dougherty, Devon. "Crisis Communications: What Every Executive Needs To Know." Walker. 1992.

[19] "Microsoft Global Security Operations Center Microsoft Uses Enterprise Incident Management Processes to Improve Security at Its Facilities." Microsoft. 13 Jul. 2012. Accessed Dec. 2012 <www.microsoft.com>.

[20] Anthonissen, Peter, ed. "Crisis Communication: Practical PR Strategies for Reputation Management & Company Survival". Kogan Page. 2008.

[21] Plowright, Teresa. "When Is Hurricane Season?" *About.com.* Accessed 6 Dec. 2012 <travelwithkids.about.com>.

[22] "Hurricane Katrina." National Climatic Data Center. 29 Dec. 2005. Accessed 8 Dec. 2012 <www.ncdc.noaa.gov>.

[23] Knabb, Richard D., Jamie R. Rhome, and Daniel P. Brown. "Tropical Cyclone Report: Hurricane Katrina." National Hurricane Center. 2005. Accessed 7 Dec 2012 <www.nhc.noaa.gov>.

[24] "Prepare for the First 72 Hours. Disaster Recovery Tip #11." Waldo Enterprise Client Group. 18 Mar. 2012. Accessed 7 Dec. 2012 <www.waldoecg.com>.

[25] A Failure Of Initiative: Final Report Of The Select Bipartisan Committee To Investigate The Preparation For And Response To Hurricane Katrina. U.S. House of Representatives, U.S. Congress. Government Printing Office. 15 Feb. 2006. Accessed 7 Dec. 2012 <www.uscg.mil>.

[26] Gheytanchi, Anahita, et al. "The Dirty Dozen: Twelve Failures Of The
    Hurricane Katrina Response And How Psychology Can Help."
    American Psychologist. 2007. Accessed 7 Dec 2012 <www.apa.org>.

[27] A Failure of Initiative.

[28] Ibid.

[29] "Hurricane Irene Hammers the Northeast." The Weather Channel. 28 Aug.
    2011. Accessed 6 Dec. 2012 <www.weather.com>.

[30] Jones, Sarah. "Irene V Katrina: The Contrasting Ideology of Obama v Bush In
    Evidence." *Politicus USA.* 28 Aug. 2011. Accessed 6 Dec. 2012
    <www.polilticususa.com>.

[31] Baylon, Jacqueline. "Hurricane Sandy Coverage: FEMA Uses Social Media to
    Keep People Informed." *Mainline Media News.* 30 Oct. 2012.
    Accessed 7 Dec. 2012 <www.mainlinemedianews.com>.

[32] Riegel, Deborah. "Four Big Management Lessons From Hurricane
    Sandy." *Forbes.* 14 Nov. 2012. Accessed 6 Dec. 2012
    <www.forbes.com>.

[33] Rockwell, Mark. "Response to Sandy Shows Katrina Lessons Mostly Learned,
    Says Former FEMA Chief." *Government Security News.* 3 Dec. 2012.
    Accessed 6 Dec. 2012 <www.gsnmagazine.com>.

BYOD: Organizational Impacts of Mobile Computing and Convergence

Rajesh Subramanian
November 2012

Abstract: *BYOD or Bring Your Own Device policy allows employees to work from anywhere and at any time using their personal or preferred devices and has seen a meteoric rise across multiple industries. Although this working environment provides flexibility to the employees and value to an enterprise, it presents several threats that can affect an enterprise financially as well as in reputation. Big corporations have undergone a seamless transition to this program in recent times while laying down a structure for other growing companies to adopt. It is important for the Chief Information Security Officer to understand the risks and security measures to be taken in order for the BYOD program to be successful.*

Introduction

BYOD or "Bring Your Own Device" refers to a business policy that allows employees the use of their preferred computing devices – like smartphones and laptops – for business purposes. This means employees are welcome to use personal devices (laptops, smartphones, tablets etc.) to connect to the corporate network to access information and application. The BYOD policy has rendered workspaces flexible, empowering employees to be mobile and giving them the right to work beyond their required hours. The continuous influx of readily improving technological devices has led to the mass adoption of smartphones, tablets, and laptops, challenging the long-standing policy of working on company-owned devices. Research firm Gartner has predicted that by 2014, 90 percent of organizations will support corporate applications on personal devices.[1] This has not only led to an increase in employee satisfaction but also reduced IT desktop costs for organizations as employees are willing to buy, maintain, and update devices in return for a one-time investment cost to be paid by the organization.[2]

In the early 1990s, executing different tasks necessitated the use of different devices. For instance, a mp3 player was needed to listen to music, whereas chores, tasks, and schedules were tracked by a PDA. An addition to this list was a bulky laptop and a camera and it seemed unlikely we would ever have a single device to suit our different needs any time soon. However, remarkable advances in technology in the last decade have made it possible to perform all the above-mentioned tasks using a single hi-tech device. Different technologies can work in synergy with each other, which improves user productivity and convenience. The introductions of the Xbox 360 and Apple TV in 2006 are perfect examples of technology convergence as it allows users to play games, listen to music, watch movies, and sports on a single "black box."

Emerging BYOD Threats

Every business decision is accompanied with a set of threats and a BYOD program is not immune from them. As outlined in the Gartner survey,[3] a BYOD program that allows access to corporate network, emails, client data etc. is a top security concern for enterprises. Overall, these risks can be classified into four areas as outlined below:

Network Risk

Example: Lack of device-visibility

When company-owned devices are used by all employees within an organization, the organization's IT practice has complete visibility of the devices connected to the network. This helps to analyze traffic and data exchanged over the Internet. As BYOD permits employees to carry their own devices (smartphones, laptops for business use), the IT practice team is unaware about the number of devices being connected to the network. As network visibility is of high importance,[4] this lack of visibility can be hazardous. For example, if a virus hits the network and all the devices connected to the network need be scanned, it is probable that some of the devices would miss out on this routine scan operation. In addition to this, the network security lines become blurred when BYOD is implemented.

Device Risk

Example: Loss of Devices

A lost or stolen device can result in an enormous financial and reputational embarrassment to an organization as the device may hold sensitive corporate information. Data lost from stolen or lost devices ranks as the top security threat as per the rankings released by Cloud Security Alliance.[5] With easy access to company emails as well as corporate intranet, company trade secrets can be easily retrieved from a misplaced device.

Application Risk

Example: Application Viruses and Malware

The Juniper "Mobile Security Strategies: Threats, Solutions & Market Forecasts 2012-2017" report revealed that a majority of employees' phones and smart devices that were connected to the corporate network were not protected by security software.[6] With an increase in mobile usage, mobile vulnerabilities have increased concurrently. Organizations are in a Catch-22 situation in deciding who is responsible for device security – the organization or the user.

Implementation Risk

Example: Weak BYOD policy

The effective implementation of the BYOD program should not only cover the technical issues mentioned above but also mandate the development of a robust implementation policy. Because corporate knowledge and data are key assets of an organization, the absence of a strong BYOD policy would fail to communicate employee expectations, thereby increasing the chances of device misuse. In addition to this, a weak policy fails to educate the user, thereby increasing vulnerability to the above-mentioned threats.

Industry BYOD Implementation

The BYOD program is becoming an exciting venture for most multinational firms, given its copious benefits. In spite of the threats identified above, its implementation of this burgeoning program needs to be strategic. The best practices outlined by Gartner for its efficacious execution entails a three-pronged approach – Secure the Device, Secure the Data and Protect the Network.[7] The manifestation of robust Mobile Device Management software optimizes functionality and security of the mobile communication network while reducing vulnerability.[8] VMware's Horizon Suite portrays that virtualization is a technique to secure data while following mobile users wherever they go.[9] IBM, on the other hand, ensures that BYOD users utilize the Lotus Traveler collaborative software that synchronizes email, contacts, and tasks with the company's Lotus Domino server.[10] Likewise, Cognizant's BYOD directed market research puts forth a holistic strategy and a set of policy guidelines that would enable the effective and efficient application of this program.[2] This deployment comprises of the right combination of Mobile Device Management (MDM), Mobile Application Management (MAM), and a Mobile Application Development Platform (MADP).[11]

Steps to be taken by a CISO to Mitigate BYOD Threats

The Chief Information Security Officer (CISO) is a senior-level executive who is responsible for the protection of organization technological assets. They are in-charge of the organization's information security program that safeguards its information infrastructure and resources. The following action items are some of the steps that a CISO must take to assuage against these threats:

- Develop a robust Risk Management program to identify, assess, and reduce risk exposure against these threats.
- Develop an Access Management hierarchy within the organization that resolves the access level granted to employees based on their roles and responsibilities.
- Identify and segregate critical and business sensitive data to a secure computing environment in order to avoid the problem of data loss or data corruption snowballing into a situation of massive chaos and humiliation for the organization.
- Ensure the existence of a disaster recovery program that enables business continuity.
- Finally, lead efforts in the development and review of a BYOD security policy, guidelines and practices.

Conclusion

While it has become typical for an organization to have separate devices for personal and professional use, Bring Your Own Device is a rising trend across multiple industries where this separation is converging. However, this new phenomenon continues to outpace security measures in place, presenting an organization with a plethora of security challenges. Although a change towards this program is tedious, it is the responsibility of the senior management within the organization to consider all variables involved to carve out a feasible plan for its implementation.

---

[1] "Gartner Reveals Top Predictions for IT Organizations and Users for 2011 and Beyond?" Gartner Research. 24 Oct. 2012. Accessed Nov. 2012 <www.gartner.com>

[2] "Making BYOD Work for Your Organization." Cognizant. Jun. 2012. Accessed Nov. 2012 <www.cognizant.com>.

[3] "Gartner Survey Shows BYOD Is Top Concern for Enterprise Mobile Security." Gartner Research. 14 Jun. 2012. Accessed Nov. 2012 <www.gartner.com>.

[4] Grajek, Garret. Five BYOD Threats you Must Solve Today - or Risk Losing Your Job." SC Market Scope. 22 Jun. 2012. Accessed Nov. 2012 <www.scmarketscope.com>.

[5] "Data Loss From Missing Mobile Devices Ranks as top Mobile Device Threat by Enterprises." Cloud Security Alliance. 4 Oct. 2012. Accessed Nov. 2012 <www.cloudsecurityalliance.org>.

[6] "Malware Incidents Forecast to Increase as 95 percent of Smartphones & Tablets Remain Unprotected with Security Software." Juniper Research. 25 Sept. 2012. Accessed Nov. 2012 <www.juniperresearch.com>.

[7] "iPad and Beyond: Bring Your Own Device." Gartner Research. n.d. Accessed <www.gartner.com>

[8] Finneran, Michael. "BYOD Requires Mobile Device Management. InformationWeek Mobility." Information Week. 7 May 2012. Accessed Nov. 2012 <www.informationweek.com>.

[9] Babcock, Charles. "VMware Shows More Of BYOD, Virtual Desktop Tools."
     Information Week. 29 Aug. 2012. Accessed Nov. 2012
     <www.informationweek.com>.

[10] Kanaracus, Chris. "IBM CIO Discusses Big Blue's BYOD Strategy." *PCWorld.*
      26 Mar. 2012. Accessed Nov. 2012 <www.pcworld.com>.

Department of Veterans Affairs – Current Challenges, Risks & Mitigation Strategies

Chitra Raman

June 2013

Abstract – *With a growing number of veterans stemming from U.S. conflicts in the Middle East, how the country provides for service-men and women is a critical topic. Chitra examines the current challenges facing the Department of Veterans Affairs, particularly the difficulties with processing the claim backlog and the transition to a new online system. Chitra recommends ways for the VA to tackle the daunting task of working through the backlog and successfully transitioning to the new benefits management system.*

Introduction

The U.S. mixed history with armed conflict and its self-prescribed role as a proliferator of democratic values, especially after its rise as a superpower, has led to numerous wars – most recently in Afghanistan and Iraq. Consequently, the need to take care of its veterans was recognized early on, but as a separate organization accountable to the president was only created in 1989. The U.S. Department of Veteran Affairs (VA) was tasked with taking care of the physical and mental health of veterans by maintaining health records and distributing benefits to veterans in need of treatment.

The VA has been ramping up its operation at an increasing pace and has processed over a million claims each over the last three years.[1] Still they face an increasing backlog, which has risen from 60 percent of all claims filed in 2011 to 66 percent in 2012.[2] The escalating backlog is because of the two current conflicts in the last decade and a recent decision to add three medical conditions to the list of conditions eligible for benefits. This led to the reopening of all rejected claims retrospectively. The VA is faced with the immediate challenge of handling this backlog in an expeditious manner without reducing the quality of service and care to veterans.

In response to the challenge emanating from the growing backlog of claims, the VA has set out an ambitious plan to eliminate the backlog by the year 2015.[3] The changes suggested are oriented towards transitioning to a paperless claims and benefits management process, which will increase the processing capacity of the VA. The current average time for processing claims is 240 days and the Veterans Benefit Management System aims to reduce that to 119 days.[4] As such, the VA has set an ambitious target for improving its quality of service to veterans. Unfortunately, the VA faces an immense challenge of avoiding a degradation of current operations as more resources are allocated to the transition to a computerized system. Ultimately, the long-term welfare of veterans justifies this tough transition. Unless this challenge is managed effectively, however, it could lead to reduced legislative support for this transformation plan and cause more delays in the disbursement of benefits to veterans.

The VA is facing challenges from its partner agencies as well. The U.S. Department of Defense (DOD) operates the Armed Forces Health Longitudinal Technology Application (AHLTA) system, designed to track the patient history of armed forces personnel from the time of admission to discharge from service. The DOD possesses the electronic medical health records of military personnel, including veterans, which can be used to vet the claims filed with the VA as well as provide accurate health-counseling advice. The VA uses a separate application called Veterans Health Information Systems and Technology Architecture (VistA) system, which houses the medical records of veterans after they come under the care of the VA. There have been many attempts to collaborate and integrate these two systems so that the data complements each other and facilitates the benefits disbursal process. Both departments have failed to implement the processes necessary for such a seamless integration. This forms another operational bottleneck, which reduces the throughput and the quality of care received by veterans.

Finally, the challenge that looms because of the backlog is the risk of reduced compliance to regulatory policies and due diligence. The political pressure on VA to reduce the backlog could lead to a lowering of the evaluation criteria, which might in turn lead to fraudulent claims slipping through in larger numbers.

These challenges expose the VA to risks that threaten the welfare of veterans and bring to question the capability of the VA to execute its mandate responsibly. A risk identification analysis on these challenges brings forth high, medium and low risks, which the VA must address immediately.

Strategic Impact Due to Veteran alienation and Limited User Adoption: High

One of the strategic risks facing the VA is the alienation of the direct stakeholders - the veterans who are supposed to benefit from the program. Nearly 594,000 (70 percent) of the 850,000 pending claims are queued with a processing time of more than 125 days.[5] Consequently, the veterans who require immediate attention due to acute illness or financial duress are denied help when they need it the most. The dissatisfaction among veterans regarding the status quo is reflected in the rising number of litigation against the VA.[6] These stories cause political turbulence, diminish trust, and ultimately have legal implications, which are a huge drain on the VA from a morale and financial perspective. The VA has touted the Veteran Benefits Management System as the silver bullet, which will eliminate the backlog. This plan might not solve the problem unless it encompasses a strategy to encourage user adoption of these systems. Data indicates that 64 percent of the veterans who made claims in 2010 were above the age of 65.[7] These veterans are entrenched in the current system and may be averse to the adoption of new systems. Without widespread adoption, the VA will be forced to accept paper claims, resulting in the operational maintenance of dual workflows with redundant staff and resource allocations.

Information Security and External Risks: Moderate
Another operational risk emanates from the fact that during the system transition, the VA is tasked with digitizing all the paper claims. Since this is a lengthy process, all new and supplemental claims will be accepted via the online Veteran Benefit Management System. Until the digitization is completed, supplemental claims, which are 61 percent of all

claims, will not be processed any faster than if it had been made on paper. The primary reason is that supplemental claims historically use the documents and records from the original claim and, as such, if those records are still not digitized, the workflow will continue to have the existing paperwork bottleneck. At a time when the VA will be trying to get stakeholder buy-in by showing the benefits of the new online system, such sub-optimal performance indicators may draw more skepticism and consequently resistance to change.

The VA will be faced with technological risks on two fronts. First, they are faced with the digitization of millions of documents. There is an inherent risk of data integrity and information security since it will be a challenging task to ensure that the digital records are accurate and secure. Second, they are faced with inherent bottlenecks in workflows because of the dependence on external applications like AHLTA, which is operated by the DOD. Previous attempts to integrate the two applications operated by the VA and DOD have not gone well due to bureaucratic tussles.[8] This has led to a situation where it takes up to 175 days for the DOD to send data to the VA after a request has been made.[9] This external risk has the potential of crippling the VA's ambition of reducing the backlog by 2015. The VA must integrate its application with the DOD seamlessly or minimize dependency on the DOD to levels that will not hamper its own operations.

Governance Oversight: Low

New legislation like the Stolen Valor Act indicate a growing concern among legislators that unscrupulous elements are trying to wrongly benefit from the veteran benefits program operated by the VA. Though there is not any data to suggest that many fraudulent claims are slipping through the cracks, the VA is at risk of falling victim to fraud if it lowers it guard. Since it is going through a transition and is under a lot of political pressure to meet its goal, it is especially vulnerable to lapses in diligence and not following its own governance policies in an effort to reduce the backlog faster.

Recommendations

The VA should focus on a strategy that exposes risks early in the transition process. The new system rollout plan should follow a phased approach where the results of the pilot phase can be evaluated. Staff and end-user training, as well as awareness programs, can only be effective if they are continuously improved by integrating feedback. Based on the experience of the initial roll out, the plans can be adapted for greater effectiveness and impact. The VA should consider accepting only new claims in the online system at least until all paper records are digitized. This will ensure that supplemental claims are not stuck in the backlog despite being filed online. Overall, the VA has a robust plan to transform its operations to meet the growing demand and should be successful if it mitigates the risks identified in this analysis.

---

[1] *Strategic Plan to Eliminate the Compensation Claims Backlog.* Veterans Benefits Administration, U.S. Department of Veterans Affairs. 25 Jan. 2013. Accessed <www.benefits.va.gov>

[2] *2012 VA Performance and Accountability Report.* Veterans Benefits Administration, U.S. Department of Veterans Affairs. 15 Nov. 2012. Accessed <www.benefits.va.gov>

[3] Ibid.

[4] Emily Cole, "VA Paperless Benefits Rollout Gains Speed." *FCW.* 4 Feb. 2013. Accessed <www.fcw.com>.

[5] Strategic Plan to Eliminate the Compensation Claims Backlog.

[6] Abramson, Larry, "VA Struggles to Provide Vets With Mental Health Care." *National Public Radio.* 25 Apr. 2012. Accessed <www.npr.org>.

[7] "Recipient Population Is Changing, and Awareness Could Be Improved." U.S. Government Accountability Office, Dec. 2011. Accessed <www.gao.gov>.

[8] Munnecke, Tom, "VistA and AHLTA on the Daily Show", *Tom Munnecke's Eclectica,* 3 May 2013. Accessed <munnecke.com>

[9] Patricia Kime, "DoD Chastised for Role in VA Claims Backlog." *Military Times.* 16 Apr. 2013. Accessed <www.militarytimes.com>.

Bridging the Digital Divide - The African Condition

Del Hazeley

June 2013

Abstract: *While affecting every part of the world, the effect of the digital divide on the continent of Africa is more pervasive and dire than in any other region. Attempts by external stakeholders are being made and sparks of innovation across the continent have been witnessed in the effort to bridge the divide, however they have proved insufficient in matching the pace of technological innovations in the developed world due to the underlying challenges facing the continent. The African Manifesto for Science, Technology, and Innovation recognizes these challenges and presents a roadmap to a technologically independent Africa. In response to the manifesto's call for enhancements, this research note reviews the key tenets of the document and seeks to augment it further by offering concepts with which the foundational impediments preventing the continent from bridging the digital divide can be overcome.*

The digital divide, is understood to be "the gap between those who do and those who do not have access" to digital technology, computers, and the Internet[1] wherein the term access is defined as the motivational, material, mastery and manipulative access to technology. Depending on the discipline or perspective of the subject, the digital divide could refer to the inequality of accessing and using these technologies within a local community or the more global issue pertaining to the gross inequality of accessibility and usage between the developed world and that of developing nations. Due to the broad nature of this concept and the brevity required within this research note, some specificity is required before proceeding. The digital divide in developed worlds is, more often than not, a concern of the 'haves' and the 'have-latters.'[2] A problem that, while noteworthy, may be better categorized as digital latency rather than a true divide. The focus moving forward therefore will be on the latter concern, regarding the inability to utilize technology in developing countries to allow for innovation. Dissimilar to the issue of digital latency, the notion of the digital divide in this instance is amplified due to the substantial delay of technologies and its magnified scope.

This research note seeks to address this disproportionate utilization of technology to further innovation in developing countries compared to that of the developed world, a more accurate digital divide. Although the concepts that follow are applicable to regions that could be categorized as 'developing,' the continent of Africa will serve as the context for this research note due to the broader impact across the continent as a whole. While acknowledging that Africa is a vast continent, with countries that number almost three scores, the research note will refer to the continent as one due to the reality that the divide spreads across its entire span, with limited exceptions. The continent of Africa, the second largest in the world, is arguably one of the worlds' least technologically advanced. Currently, there is a minute fraction of countries across the 54-nation continent, which can be considered innovative in terms of technological prowess, however even within those nations innovations are segmented to but a few cities.

Admittedly there are a multitude of factors that gradually led to the continent's digital divide however two key deficiencies are most prominent as the cause of the increasing wedge. A lack of knowledge or ability to develop technological solutions independently (mastery) and the insufficient infrastructure with which to create or support technologies (material) has drifted the continent apart from the developed world in terms of technological innovations. In a world where information is power and innovation the tool with which to wield it, the continent can ill afford to continue its reliance on the knowledge and resources of the developed world.

According to a United Nations Educational, Scientific and Cultural Organization report "38 percent of the adult population in sub-Saharan Africa, or 153 million adults, lack the basic literacy and numeracy skills needed in everyday life."[3] This is a number five times greater than that of the U.S.[4] The infrastructural landscape is equally bleak. An Africa Infrastructure Country Diagnostic report commissioned by the World Bank[5] states that electrical power is the continent's largest infrastructure challenge. The report also notes the lack of telecommunications, poor water handling capacities, and inadequate transportation networks across the continent.

This issue is not novel and is one that external parties looking in have attempted to resolve by implementing initiatives to address the rift. Such initiatives as One Laptop Per Child (OLPC), which sought to deliver subsidized laptops to the continent, attempted to bridge the divide through aid. However in most cases within the continent, it encountered educational and infrastructural challenges[6] whereby the devices could either not be electrically sustained or wherein teachers didn't have the necessary skills to leverage the device in the classroom. Another such initiative was an information and communications technology for development (ICT4D) initiative, which deployed 'telecenters' in the hopes of making distance education and telemedicine a reality. However, it too encountered similar challenges whereby either the services were used for ulterior motives over the pursuit of knowledge or wherein the infrastructure could not be supported long term.[7] While these are but a few examples, the trend is one of recurrence for such initiatives deployed to bridge the divide, which while well intentioned, primarily focus on one deficiency without addressing the other.

When examined closely, the primary misjudgment that affects these initiatives deployed by external stakeholders is the expectation that they can be done without fully understanding the local context within which they will be implemented. This is often the result of an absence of situational awareness or overwhelming assurance in the ability to overcome the educational and infrastructural challenges by sheer force of will. For instance, deploying computers in regions where there is no established infrastructure, schooling is poor, and similar critical concerns are unaddressed is akin to putting the cart before horse, to borrow a classic idiom. Implementation of such initiatives after first consulting local experts, not necessarily in the field of technology, to either serve as counselors or intermediaries could have served the function of informing the decision on how best to implement the initiative, specific to that community, thereby increasing the chance of success while also potentially providing a socioeconomic boost to the region.

When local solutions are developed to address local problems, the results are quite impressive. For example, Kenyan owned Safaricom released M-Pesa[8] a mobile payment system operating outside of the traditional banking system has been touted as a mobile banking catalyst for its unique conglomeration of features. Uchaguzi, a derivative of the Ushahidi platform,[9] is a crowdsourcing platform that was instrumental in seeing the 2013 Kenyan elections to a peaceful result, an antithesis of the country's previous general elections. Another innovation, which many in the tech industry and even those not on the continent may be familiar with is Ubuntu.[10] The enterprise-grade server platform developed in 2004 is currently one of the world's premier open source operating systems. These innovations originating from the continent, which have been of significant value to its local population and even beyond, are exemplary not only of the benefits of locally developed technologies but also the potential of African innovation.

Regrettably, these instances, while exceptional, are typically isolated and quite infrequent. As mentioned previously, these innovations occur in but a fraction of the continent and are found in only few key locations, such as capital cities and major business hubs of a handful of countries. Unfortunately, some ignore that reality and point to them as proof that this digital divide is merely a further decelerated version of digital latency. To substantiate this claim, they may point to the proliferation of mobile technology across the continent, touting statistics of mobile phones outselling computers at a ratio of 4-to-1 and indicating that over half of the Internet connections across the continent are exclusively mobile[11] as signs of progression. The reality is that while a 65 percent penetration of mobile across Africa has certainly had a social impact on the continent through the exposure of injustices[12] and mobilization of peoples leveraging social media,[13] it is worth noting that the division remains vast since mobile phones inherently bear limitations in the software and hardware of the technology. The benefits of the ICT platform, past the social value that it provides, become isolated to the app builders and service vendors. This therefore only serves to perpetuate the cycle of technological dependency rather than self-sustainability and innovation.

Bridging the digital divide can be done neither by simply infusing technology into the continent nor by the propagation of these technological 'walled gardens.' To earnestly bridge the divide, an environment must be developed in which innovation thrives, one that empowers Africans to develop homegrown innovations that address African needs and do so with more frequency and rampancy than currently exists. This is essential, to replace the need for aid infusions by external stakeholders, however well intentioned, that are often either truly unexposed to the needs of Africans or detached from the genuine interests of the continent. It is in the awareness of this need that the *African Manifesto for Science, Technology, and Innovation*[14] was developed. The manifesto, declared as "a tool for shaping shared visions about science, technology and innovation (STI) in Africa, for Africans, by Africans, in a multi-lateral dialogue, with the rest of the world" provides a framework with which African nations and regions can begin to design governmental policies to bridge the divide.

The architects of the manifesto sought to provoke a living dialogue among Africans, who bear the responsibility to bridge the divide, and urge the sharing of ideas in contribution to the document. It is in response to this call that this author seeks to evaluate the manifesto's potency in truly alleviating the aforementioned deficiencies, following a deconstruction of the suppositions raised, and enhancing the document where necessary in the interests of providing a more robust framework. One which pan-African policies, that create an environment primed for technological innovation, can be established.

With regards to the educational deficiency and the need to develop Africa's knowledge, especially in the realm of science and technology, the manifesto offers considerable insight into the circumstances that brought about the status quo and provides a broad direction to which Africans must move towards to overcome the shortcoming. Firstly, the Manifesto duly exposes the knowledge dependence in which Africans currently exist, a trickle-down position that has resulted in Africa's constant race to catch-up. In terms of potential for growth, the report says that the "have"s and the "have-not"s has become synonymous with the "know"s and the "know-not"s. It calls for the investment in academia and research to foster innovation while also noting that Africans should strive to create their own unique innovations rather than imitating that of the developed world's since for implementations to be effective, they must be "fully embedded in Africa's societies, cultures and human experiences," a criteria neither the OLPC nor some of the ICT4D deployments could accomplish. While not specifically outlining the manner by which the

educational gap can be improved, it does call for an
increase in governmental allocation to these interests.

Investing in research and higher education is certainly
a step in the right direction, and essentially, this
endowment is crucial to continued innovation.
However, adjoined to this idea needs to be the focus
on improving the primary and secondary school
systems which form the cornerstone with which a
bridge to span the digital divide can be built. Science,
Technology, Engineering, and Math (STEM) must be
integrated at every level since cultivation during this
period is vital in developing an innovative mind.
Young minds are especially adept at 'thinking outside
the box' and in them rests the continent's hope of
furthering the innovation that this generation shall
begin and even overcome challenges that were
previously presumed insurmountable. This however
relies on proper investment in the schools, teachers,
and curriculum to build outstanding students. The
continent could look inwards at the examples set by
Mauritius and South Africa, which have strengthened
their investments in education and seeing the
socioeconomic boost it brings.

In addition, strategies should also be enacted that seek
to expose the innovative amongst us. The Manifesto
speaks to the recognition of an "African Head of State
or Head of Parliament who has demonstrated strong

and visible leadership for [science, technology and innovation]" but explicitly deprecates the awarding of such 'prize' to scientists. This however is the first point of contention. Such acknowledgment is instead best designed around the merits of the Nobel Prize, which is awarded to the innovator rather than the facilitator of such innovation. If prizes must be awarded to the Heads, a better strategy would be to base it off separate distinctions and whenever possible awarded to alternate countries, to strengthen its effect. Exposing the continent's innovators allows cross-boundary collaboration to further build on currently disbursed knowledge and expertise in education, innovation, and policymaking.

Implementing these means to technological mastery however requires the material to create and support it, and this is an issue, which the Manifesto addressed poorly. While acknowledging that "the human and physical infrastructure" are in "very bad shape," it proposes that to "build these infrastructures requires devoting consistently a high proportion of the national budget to higher education and improving the incentive structure for scientists and innovators." This prioritization of higher education and research would be accurate save for the oversight that scientists and innovators would still be hindered by the limitations of the existing infrastructure.

Hypothetically, even if Africa's leaders were to ignore the rest of the population and focus on this privileged cluster, an unreliable power supply and scant telecommunications cabling channeling less than optimal data speeds ensures very little, if any, innovative research can be executed.

This should be seen as a call for equal investment in the critical infrastructure that this research relies on, not as a desire to cut funding to critical research. Investing in reliable power grids and robust telecommunications ensures that critical research is maintained while also increasing the wellbeing of the general citizenry. This also increases the potential for the serendipitous innovation that is possible when the public at large has access to innovative resources. As the Manifesto, in summation, appeals in its "call to action" we must "reject knowledge dependence" and this is not done by simply relying on the ICT benefits that mobile communication brings to the continent but to invest in the physical infrastructure that supports the development of African-focused software and hardware. Appealing for "bottom-up innovation," similarly, does not occur by awarding Heads of States but rather by empowering the masses to innovate. Ushahidi, mentioned earlier, was developed in an "open Space for technologists, investors, tech companies and hackers in Nairobi."[15]

The continent requires additional investment in such facilities most urgently while the rest of its infrastructure matures.

While the deployment of the material access that makes this technological innovation possible is being implemented quite late, relative to developed worlds, and the mastery of these tools has been primarily scattered in pockets across the continent. Only recently has it been developed in a broader effort. An initial disadvantage, to be certain, however leaves the continent in a prospectively favorable position to learn from the mistakes made by the technological trendsetters and leveraging that status to leapfrog the technologies of the developed world. Harvard professor, Calestous Jumas states, "Africa's potential for transforming itself and the world market through emerging technologies lies in the very nature of being a latecomer."[16] This potential has caught the eye of major technology players in the developed world seeking financial growth. Companies such as IBM, Orange™, and Baidu, to name a few, are all focused on the continent and its untapped population.[17] Africa should examine these interests with caution and effectively assess the benefits and risks of each company before engaging in trade. Negotiations must embody an investment in the growth of the continent and knowledge transference, long term, lest it faces a renewed period of exploitation.

Holistically, the Manifesto presents strong evidence for the need for Africa, as whole, to rely on self-innovation through collaboration if it wishes to bridge the digital divide. The recommendations supplied by the Manifesto require further refinement, as the authors readily confess, but offer an excellent foundation for policy development. The true power of the document is in its potential to stir discourse among technologists and leaders in the continent, the first and arguably most critical step in building the mastery and material infrastructure Africans need to bridge the divide. Historically "Africa has numerous initiatives started, stalled, abandoned and gone to waste in the past"[18] however due to the urgency and importance of bridging the divide, this is a practice the continent can ill afford to continue. The onus is on regional African organizations such as the Economic Community of West African States[19] in partnership with pan-African organizations such as the African Union[20] to increase oversight and strive to maintain stability across the continent to ensure the interests of the continent are paramount. Pan-African groups must also set broad guidelines and values for which the continent as a whole should strive to accomplish with a vision of where the continent should be in at a certain future target. Because he regional groups are focused and representative of the needs of each specific region, they can create more stringent policies based on the pan-African agenda. This may encourage continued development of the material and mastery infrastructure that enables innovation. These policies must be accompanied with detailed roadmaps to gauge success throughout its progression because failure to plan is a plan to fail, to cite the popular adage.

A concluding addendum to the Manifesto is on the application of the over 100,000 'highly educated' African migrants the continent has lost.[21] As a result of past instabilities, and individuals in search of better education and jobs, the continent has suffered from considerable 'brain drain.' The renewed effort for bridging this divide should lean on these experts that have a connection to Africa, not only for their input in policy making but also in directly supporting the continent in its effort to address the deficiencies it is laden with, especially that of mastery.

The expanse is vast, and the project challenging, however it is not impossible. *The African Manifesto for Science, Technology and Innovation* lays out a sound framework with which governmental policies can be developed. As requested by the writers of the document, it has been reviewed for reinforcement where appropriate and reevaluation where needed. The true labor however is yet to be done. Africans, home and away, must unshackle themselves from the physical and psychological confines formed in the colonial era and unilaterally answer this call to service. This digital divide must be bridged with all deliberate speed.

[1] Van Dijk, Jan AGM. The Deepening Divide: Inequality in the Information
          Society. Sage
Publications, Inc. Feb. 2005.

[2] Baase, Sara. A Gift of Fire: Social, Legal, and Ethical Issues for Computing
          Technology. Prentice Hall. 5 Aug. 2012.

[3] Reaching the Marginalized - Education for All Global Monitoring Report 2010.
          UNESCO. 2010. Accessed <www.unesco.org>

[4] Dunn, Jeff. "The Current State Of Literacy In America." *Edudemic
          Informational*. 13 Nov. 2012.
Accessed 11 Mar. 2013 <www.edudemic.com>.

[5] *Africa's Infrastructure: A Time for Transformation*. The World Bank. 2010.
          Accessed 11 Mar. 2013 <www.worldbank.org>.

[6] Nsanzimana, Jean-Christophe. "Rwanda: MPs Fault Mineduc On OLPC
          Shortcomings." Rwanda
Focus. 4 Mar. 2013. Accessed 11 Mar. 2013.

[7] Toyama, Kentaro. "Can Technology End Poverty?" *Boston Review*. Dec. 2010.
          Accessed 8 Feb.
2013.

[8] "M-PESA Timeline." Safaricom. 2012. Accessed <www.safaricom.co.ke>.

[9] "Ushahidi." Ushahidi. 2012. Accessed 6 Dec. 2012 <www.ushahidi.com>.

[10] "The Ubuntu Story." Ubuntu. 2013. Accessed 11 Mar. 2013
          <www.ubuntu.com>.

[11] *Spotlight on Africa - Mobile Statistics & Facts 2012*. Praekelt Foundation. 16
          Jul. 2012. Accessed Mar. 2013 <www.blog.praekeltfoundation.org>.

[12] "S Africa Police Hit by 'Dragging Video'." Feb. 2013. Al Jazeera. Accessed 5
        Mar. 2013 <www.aljazerra.com>.

[13] Gustin, Sam. "Social Media Sparked, Accelerated Egypt's Revolutionary Fire."
        Wired Business.

Feb. 2011. Accessed 11 Mar. 2013 <www.wired.com>.

[14] *The African Manifesto for Science, Technology and Innovation*. African
        Technology Policy Studies Network. 2010. Accessed Mar. 2013
        <www.atpsnet.org>.

[15] "IHub." iHub. N.d. Accessed 6 Dec. 2012 <www.ihub.co.ke>.

[16] Jumas, Calestous. "Trading Places: Commerce Drives Science And
        Technology In Africa –

Forbes." *Forbes*. Nov. 2012. Accessed 7 Mar. 2013 <www.forbes.com>.

[17] "Information Technology in Africa: The Next Frontier." *The Economist*. 16th
        Feb. 2013. Accessed 9 Mar. 2013 <www.economist.com>.

[18] Nyong', Peter Anyang'. *Technology and Innovation in Africa*. The African
        Leadership Forum. 4 Aug. 2011. Accessed
        <www.africaconvention.org>.

[19] "ECOWAS Commission at a Glance." The Economic Community Of West
        African States. 2007. Accessed Mar. 2013 <www.comm.ecowas.int>.

[20] "AU In a Nutshell." African Union. n.d. Accessed <www.au.int>.

[21] Carrington, William J., and Enrica Detragiache. "How Extensive Is the Brain
        Drain?" *Finance*

& Development. International Monetary Fund. Jun. 1999. Accessed
        <www.imf.org>.